Settling for Less Than God's Best?

A Relationship Checkup for Single Women

Elsa Kok

New Hope Publishers

Birmingham, Alabama

New Hope® Publishers
P. O. Box 12065
Birmingham, AL 35202-2065
www.newhopepubl.com

Library of Congress Cataloging-in-Publication Data

Kok, Elsa, 1968-
  Settling for less than God's best? : a relationship checkup for single women / Elsa Kok.
    p. cm.
  ISBN 1-56309-750-8 (softcover)
  1. Single women—Religious life. 2. Christian women—Religious life.
3. Mate selection—Religious aspects—Christianity. 4. Dating (Social customs)—Religious aspects—Christianity. I. Title.
  BV4596.S5 K64 2003
  248.8'432—dc21
                        2002151205

Cover design by Righteous Planet Design, Inc.
    Franklin, Tennessee

ISBN: 1-56309-750-8

N034112 • 1206 • 7.5C2

Settling for Less Than God's Best?

Dedication

This book is dedicated to my daughter

Samantha Kelly Lynch.

May you choose God's best in every area of your life.
May you trust in His love and believe in His promises.
And may you never forget how much you are loved.

Table of Contents

Acknowledgments

Abundant thanks and praise to Jesus Christ, who has again allowed me the privilege of sharing from my brokenness in order to direct hearts toward Him. What an incredible honor! I love you, Jesus.

I have to thank my family. Every one of them. Dad, for your great humor and wisdom. Mom, for your heart of prayer and your sweet encouragement. My brothers: Piet, Enno, Rob, and John—I love you. Thank you for looking out for Sami and me in so many different ways. To Carol, Laura, and Wendy—you are sisters. Not in-laws or by law, but in love. I am so grateful for you.

To the women who shared their stories to make it happen: Thank you for being vulnerable and exposing your lives. You made this real . . . Rachelle G., Susan T., Gwen C., Leslie C., Julie S., Deb W., Barbara A., Carol K., Amy M., Jane H., Becky D., Jennifer B., Cindy M., Denise M., Denise G., Sandy B., Erin S., Lauren F., Gretchen A., Jan P., Bobbi E., Lacey M., Cara H., Sherry T., and the many others who poured pieces of themselves into this manuscript, thank you!

To Jennifer Briner—My dear friend and prayer partner, I love you. Thank you for holding me accountable to the truth and for always revealing God's heart to me. And for reading every single chapter in the middle of your own full life. Wow!

To the VanWaardes—I love you more than words can say. Your home was a safe place for me, a refuge when things seemed bigger than I could bear. Carol, sharing tea and conversation will always be a sweet memory. Piet, thank you for reading the book and always believing in me . . . and entrusting me with ministry tasks. That was huge. For Pieter, Mallory, and Curran—you bring tremendous joy to me. Thank you.

The incredible women at New Hope—Thank you for walking me through every step of this process, for answering my questions, hearing my thoughts, and seeking to give it all your best. It's been such a pleasure to work with you.

Thom Bolden—You have always been there for me. No matter what emergency came screeching my way, you put your own stuff down and came to help. Thank you so much.

Susan Trice—What awesome counsel you gave. Thank you for your support and your wonderful editing skills. You were a big part of this!

Denise Gray—Thank you for reading through each chapter and giving me such good things to think about. I love you!

Jane Henke—Thank you also for reading through this book and for your awesome encouragement every step of the way.

Janie Magruder—I love you so much. Thank you for the many ways you support and encourage me. Your love makes a difference in my life!

Deb Waggoner—You're my hero. Thanks for serving with the heart of God.

Bob McNear—Thank you for introducing me to the kind of melt-in-your-mouth ice cream that I never even knew existed. Thanks for loving God with such tenderness.

And I pray, out of the kindness of my own heart, that your life may be free from all forms of lawn art. Wahoo! Thanks for everything, Bob—more than simple words can express.

Teresa Parker—Thanks for publishing my very first article way back when. You're such a sweet encourager!

Laura Talbert and Cara Horn—How fun it's been to serve with you, to walk through several years together. Thanks for your friendship.

Micah and Robin—I love you both so much. Your growth and hunger for God inspire me!

Donna, Cheryl, Marilee, Kay, Debi, Lucy, Deb, Shari, Sherry, Becky, Bev, Ellen, Jeannie, Heather, Shari, and to the rest of the WEB ladies—You have been such a huge part of my journey. May God pour back into you by the boatload!

Ray Scott—For kind and continual and sweet support, thank you.

Gretchen—Thanks for making me laugh in all the best ways. You are an amazing woman, talented and beautiful and real. Thanks.

And to the Sunday crew—Athir, Julie, Jason, Matt, Laura, Shari, Casey, Kim, Charlie, Kari . . . thank you for your love, prayers and encouragement.

Brittany—To one of the coolest teenagers I know. Stand strong and hold fast—God has a special plan for your life!

Susan Goodwin Graham—Thank you for being a woman of God—you are beautiful inside and out!

Reeses—The dog. Have to thank him, he's put up with me the most of everyone. And he still pants and grins and loves me with every enthusiastic wag. When I look at that furry face, I'm reminded that God must be playful and fun. Thank you Reeses.

Introduction

I think of you as my friend. I see you in the faces of the ladies at my church, the young women at the coffee shop, the single parents of my community. I see the same yearnings and desires to know godly love and true companionship. It's a wish we all share, a longing we all know in the deepest parts of our souls. I pray that this book helps to bring you closer to the knowledge of sweet relationship.

I've read a thousand books (okay, slight exaggeration) on dating and sifted through them to discover the most biblically accurate counsel I could find. I write of my experiences and share pieces of my broken relational past, all in hopes of giving you a roadmap to joy in relationship.

I am one of you. I don't have a doctorate in counseling, nor am I a dating professional. I was a young adult who knew butterflies and weak knees when I fell in love for the first time. I was a twenty-something-year-old who survived a broken marriage, and I remain a single mother who has been on her own for the last nine years. I'm not writing from the comfort of a marriage relationship but from the battlefield of singleness.

Basically, I know what you're going through. I've fought through temptation, frustration, dependence, and dating anxiety. I've learned a tremendous amount and expect to learn more as God continues His work in me. It hasn't been easy. I've done the broken-hearted, chocolate-eating, late-into-the-night-crying over broken relationships. I've danced around like a teenager in love. I've handled relationships well. I've handled them poorly. And I've grown.

Oh, how I pray for you! I pray that God will minister to you through each and every chapter. I pray that you will be honest with yourself when you catch sight of a red flag, and I pray that you will celebrate when you encounter a green light. I pray that past brokenness won't rob you of future joy. I pray that if this is your first journey into the realm of love and relationship, this book will equip you to know success. Most of all, I hope that you will know and believe and trust that God has a *best* for you. He loves you and knows exactly what you need when you need it. He is the most romantic of all and He is the Giver of all good gifts. Trust Him! Oh, that you may find joyful rest in Him as you take a close look at your relationships.

All my best to you, my lady friends. We're in this together. May God bless us all as we seek first after His heart and His best for us!

In prayer for you,
Elsa Kok

Chapter One
Desires of Your Heart

Men are wonderful. I've always been partial to them. My appreciation dates back to the third grade, when I first encountered a boy named Louis. He was tall for his age, as was I. He had dark, curly hair and an impish smile that set my little heart aflutter. I had it all planned out. He would ask me to the school fair at the end of the year, and I would be his forever. In my mind it was all very simple.

I invited Louis to my house to play one afternoon. I instructed him that on the following day, we would hold hands. Our class was scheduled to watch a movie. To reduce suspicion, I told him that I would enter first while he would come in toward the end of the line. I would sit in the back of the room, he would come join me, and once the film started . . . voila. Our romance would begin. We practiced in my room and he seemed to have it down. Until the next day. I entered the room and sat at the back of the classroom. Several children later, Louis entered. He looked at me, there in the back, and proceeded to sit as far forward as he possibly could.

And so was my introduction to the world of romance.

My longings didn't change much over the years. I went

from wanting someone to hold my hand to wanting someone to be there for me, to talk with me, to hold me close.

When I was sixteen I met Darren. He lived far away and we started a correspondence. The letters we wrote became a romantic story of their own. His middle name is Earl, so I dubbed him Prince Earl. My full name is Elizabeth; He dubbed me Queen Elizabeth. We wrote letters as Prince Earl (of a distant magical kingdom) and Queen Elizabeth. Our letters spoke of dragons, valiant battles, and romantic escapades. The romantic fiction we created intertwined with the genuine longings and desires of our hearts. He truly wanted to be the valiant prince. I wanted, more than anything, to be a coveted queen. And in our stories, we were everything we dreamed of.

I loved Darren. He was my world. I once said to him, "Love isn't a strong enough word . . . I adore you!" I wanted to spend the rest of my life as Queen Elizabeth, protected and loved by the courageous prince. Nothing else mattered to me. I lied to my parents. I skipped school and stowed away on trains to visit him. I gave him not only my heart but also my body. I knew that he was the "forever man" for me, the one who would love me until death did us part. Not a single doubt did I have about our future . . . until that summer evening when he told me it was over.

I sobbed. I spent years pining for his devotion, certain that someday things would return to what they had once been.

They never did. And the longing remained. I tried to fill the hole in my heart with other men. Always the desire remained that someone out there was destined to be "the one." The next one would be it, the man to love and cherish me, the one I would love and encourage and support to greatness. I knew it was bound to happen, and my need drove me to look everywhere I went. I would get into a relationship, give my everything, only to be disillusioned again. It would take me forever to disconnect (or be disconnected by him), and then I would search again. It seemed as though I was constantly hoping, longing, aching to be fulfilled by a man's love. My need consumed me.

The Truth About Desire

"The reason we enjoy fairy tales—more than enjoy them—the reason we identify with them in some deep part of us is because they rest on two great truths: The hero really has a heart of gold and the beloved really possesses hidden beauty," say Brent Curtis and John Eldredge in *The Sacred Romance.*

I had it all wrong. My longing for a man, for someone to love and to be loved by, was wrapped and twisted and intertwined with the longing God creates in each one of us, the longing for Him. God is the true knight, the one and only, the lover of our hearts and souls. He is the One who knows us and loves us anyway. He is the One who will never walk away, who will always pursue, who will fight until the end. I remember so clearly the desire I had for someone who would go to battle for me. "I just want someone who is willing to fight for me, to fight for us . . ." I used to lament. I yearned for a man who wouldn't give up on me, who would fight for who I was and who we were together. I didn't understand that the Someone who was willing to fight for me was the very One who created me.

No, in all these things we are more than conquerors through him who loved us. For I am convinced that neither death nor life, neither angels nor demons, neither the present nor the future, nor any powers, neither height nor depth, nor anything else in all creation, will be able to separate us from the love of God that is in Christ Jesus our Lord. —Romans 8:37–39

Never will I leave you; never will I forsake you. —Hebrews 13:5

How great is the love the Father has lavished on us, that we should be called children of God! —1 John 3:1

When you pass through the waters, I will be with you; and when you pass through the rivers, they will not sweep over you. When you walk through the fire, you will not be burned; the flames will not set you ablaze. For I am the LORD, your God, the Holy One of Israel, your Savior. —Isaiah 43:2–3

Amazing. Real. Genuine. Powerful. And there was more. The Jesus I heard about as a child, but didn't yet know as my friend, wasn't only willing to fight for me; He was willing to enter enemy territory and give His life on my behalf. "The gospel says that we, who are God's beloved, created a cosmic crisis . . . we were stolen from our True Love and that he launched the greatest campaign in the history of the world to get us back. God created us for intimacy with him. When we turned our back on him he promised to come for us. He sent personal messengers; he used beauty and affliction to recapture our hearts. After all else failed, he conceived the most daring of plans. Under the cover of night he stole into the enemy's camp incognito, the Ancient of Days disguised as a newborn," write Curtis and Eldredge.

For many of us, the longing for the One who loves us most gets focused on a human guy like Louis, who then sits at the front of the classroom to avoid our need. Or we get the longings so mixed up that we swear off men forever and stuff our hearts deep within. It is there where we feel safe because we know at some level no one will ever be able to answer the ache.

God's Desire

Some say that if we long for companionship, something must be lacking in our relationship with God. There might be a raised eyebrow, that knowing look, that subtle inference that we must not be right with God if our hearts still yearn for a mate. "Oh, once you have God, you really don't need anyone else." That's simply not true.

I truly believe that there has to be a balance in how we approach this tender subject. If we say that healthy desires are outside of God's will, then we feel guilty for longing for romance. Yet to be consumed by the hunger distracts us from the One who truly provides for our core needs.

The key is separating the two longings—our desire for God and our yearning for a mate—and putting them in order. Ultimately, God is after our hearts. He wants us to make Him our first priority. He wants to be number one in our lives, for He is a jealous God (Ex. 20:5, Deut. 4:24). This ranking of priority is not for His benefit; it's for ours. When we have our hearts tucked into His care, then we can safely love another without fear of losing everything. If God has the first and best parts of us, then no broken romance can strip away our identity and leave us wounded beyond repair.

So how do we put God first? In a society where dating is romanticized as the one thing that will make us whole again, how do we pursue God for our needs? Let's begin by taking a look at our expectation for a dating relationship. Deep within our heart of hearts, what is it that we expect to happen when "the one" comes along? If we can look at that process realistically, we will be much more willing to pursue God as the first priority in our lives.

Who Is "The One"?

"He'll be perfect," she said to me with that dreamy look in her eyes. "He'll have blond hair, blue eyes, and the perfect build." With certainty, she went on. "He'll be a believer, he'll love the outdoors, be terribly romantic, and full of wisdom. He'll love me and honor me and protect me. He'll want to talk about everything." She paused, just long enough to catch her breath. "Yes, and he'll love to cook and be willing to help with the housework. Oh, and I suppose he'll have his problems, but nothing we won't be able to work out."

I nodded. She was looking for the perfect man. And since she wasn't likely to find him this side of heaven, I had the sense my friend was heading for bitter disappointment. What about you? Perhaps you think she was a little extreme, perhaps you have a much more realistic longing. Take a look. Is it? What are you looking for? In your mind, who is the man of your dreams? Is he even human?

Just a few years ago, I had a dear guy friend ask me what I wanted in a man. I had grown as a Christian and had now settled on the other side of the spectrum from where I used to be. Rather then accepting anyone who loved me, I wanted someone with everything! I went on to list a *huge* number of things. I don't remember the exact count, but I do recall that it was pages long. I went on and on about character, godliness, similar tastes. They were all good things. What I didn't get was that no man in the world would ever be able to live up to them. I remember the list he sent back . . . it constituted five or six things, the top one being that she would love God. I was embarrassed. Much like my friend in the first paragraph, I'd disqualified everyone but Jesus.

If we have a list defined by perfection and as long as our arm, God can never grant us the desire of our heart. Because no such man exists! What happens when you go into a relationship, expecting the very best, and the man turns out to be (oh no!) human? And frail? And broken? Just like the rest of us? The truth is that while there are some things that are non-negotiable, understand that many things are not. If you understand that a man will never be able to be everything that you long for, then you will give him grace. The same grace you will need when he discovers how loudly you snore.

We'll discuss some of the non-negotiable character traits in a later chapter. For now though, take a look at your deepest longing for a mate. Is it realistic?

What About the Wedding Day?

Anne dreamed of her wedding day. Ever since she was a little girl, she had in mind what it would be like. She would walk down the aisle on her father's arm, toward her future husband. The music would catch the heart of everyone in attendance and the ambience would stir the most cavalier of souls. She would stand by the side of her beloved and commit the rest of her life to loving him. He would look in her eyes, place the ring on her finger, and together they would walk toward a future filled with laughter and romance.

Anne's visions didn't extend much beyond the wedding reception, where she pictured herself dancing in the warm embrace of her husband's strong arms. She didn't even know who that husband might be . . . she just knew what that day would look like.

When she met Zach, he seemed perfect. She fell in love . . . and she stopped there. In her heart, she didn't want to know anything more. In fact, she fought against knowing anything that might cast a shadow on their budding romance. When he asked her to marry him, she shrieked her joyful acceptance. Immediately she began planning their special day. It was all she could think about. She didn't even have time for pre-marital counseling—"There's just too much to get done."

The day was perfect. Her dress was perfect. The environment was perfect. But the marriage was not. Three weeks into her new life, with the wedding day celebration behind her, Anne discovered she was stuck. She was married. The one thing, the one moment she had lived her whole life to know, was over. All that was left was the small portion of wedding cake stuffed into her freezer and the reality of married life, which had taken her completely by surprise. She was devastated.

When you think of marriage, what comes to mind? Do you think of the romance of your wedding day? The way he will look at you as you make your way down the aisle? Please don't get me wrong. These things are not wrong, in and of themselves. But when they are our primary focus, we are bound to make poor choices. God intended that marriages last far beyond the wedding night, which means *we* need to think beyond the wedding night. They take much more work than what is involved in ordering tuxes and corsages. Knowing this can save us all kinds of heartbreak and disappointment.

It's okay to dream, my friends. It's okay to wonder what that day will be like and even to imagine a godly man at the end of the aisle. Just know that the moment awaiting you there is just the beginning of a long, hard, rewarding, amazing, wonderful journey. It is not the end, the point of arrival for any of us. It is the beginning of so much more. Knowing that helps.

But When, Exactly?

So we understand that the guy won't be perfect, and getting married is more than "you may kiss the bride." But how long do we have to wait for all of this?

He was a musician, and I'm a sucker for the musical type. Deep blue eyes, blond hair, creativity . . . *life.* He searched for my writing on the Internet, he read my stories, and he smiled at me whenever I passed by. I was on vacation, a family reunion. He worked at the place we were staying. At first I didn't really notice him—until his attentions increased. He brought me chocolate, wrote me notes, expressed how he loved my writing. Plus . . . I made him nervous. He would turn twelve shades of red whenever I came near. While eloquent on paper, in person he could barely find the words. His speechlessness charmed me.

I found myself looking for Scott whenever I stepped outside of my cabin. "I'm not really interested," I would mumble to myself as I looked anxiously around for a glimpse of the golf cart he drove around the complex.

I knew he wasn't the guy for me because of some of the things he had shared. He was in the middle of a divorce and needed his own time to heal. But how quickly my desires took over! Despite all of my growth, despite all my steps toward God and His purposes, I was melting like a teenage girl.

And I learned. Our desire for companionship can blind us to everything we hold dear. It sneaks up on us most unexpectedly, and it hits twice as hard when we are living in a place of impatience.

I didn't know that then. Besides, it felt good to be found beautiful; it felt nice to communicate with a man. I enjoyed his sidelong glances and the way he stuttered in my presence. He was endearing himself to me. I was beginning to like him, to want more time with him, even though I knew he wasn't quite right for me. God understood us well when He said in the Song of Solomon, "Daughters of Jerusalem, I charge you by the gazelles and by the does of the field; do not arouse or awaken love until it so desires." I was allowing opportunities for a relationship to build with the blue-eyed musician. I didn't see the harm in it, in the same way a fly might marvel as it takes a closer look at the beauty of a web. My desire, my longing was clouding my vision, and once I realized it, I ran with all of me to bring my feelings quickly to my heavenly Father.

The truth is, there is "no hunger so severe that it justifies trading away God's will to satisfy it," say Dennis McCallum and Gary Delashmutt in *The Myth of Romance.* I had done that before, fallen in before I knew what I was doing. I'd lost my heart because of hunger. I couldn't let that happen again.

When I brought my slip-up to God, He lovingly showed me something. I wasn't waiting on Him. I had been feeling as though enough time had passed for me alone. It had been a couple of years and I felt like I was ready to be in a relationship again. Even if it wasn't the right relationship, I felt like I had done my time. In a rush to feed my desire, I was running to the wrong person in the wrong season of my life. There was still some work God wanted to do on my heart, still some things He needed to train and develop in me. And singleness remains the perfect time to learn.

What is your time limit? If you don't meet someone by next week, next month, next year, how will you react? If God waits three years because He so longs to give you His best, will you wait? Take these to heart as you consider:

Yet the LORD longs to be gracious to you; he rises to show you compassion. For the LORD is a God of justice. Blessed are all who wait for him! —Isaiah 30:18

Wait for the LORD; be strong and take heart and wait for the LORD. —Psalm 27:14

Our God is faithful, dear ones. He longs to give us good things. We can count on Him and trust in Him.

Not All Roses and Chocolate ...

Personally, this whole desire thing was huge. I had a lot of very unrealistic desires in my heart. Not only did I want the beautiful wedding day with the good man, and soon, but also I believed deep down that marriage would fix something in me. I thought that while it might be hard, I would have arrived at this mysterious place of "everything will be okay now." Something about singleness felt so vulnerable that I was certain dating and being in love and marriage would make me all better.

When I married Billy at the tender age of twenty, I had definite ideas about what married life would look like. Even though our dating life was pretty tumultuous, I thought things would change when we were married. I had this vision of being the perfect wife married to the perfect husband producing the perfect children. I might have said something wiser and more realistic, but deep in my heart I believed that marriage was going to be a wonderful ride, a coasting toward eternal bliss. I believed that it would make me whole in ways that nothing else could.

Even when the marriage ended four years later and I was suddenly standing alone with an eighteen-month-old girl, I figured it was only because it wasn't the right marriage to the right man. Someone was still waiting out there for me; it had to be so. Someone who would make my life right, who would sweep in and bring me the joy I was longing for.

I can't tell you how discouraged I was when the truth became clear to me. And it took years for that to happen! I stubbornly held on to the dream of my knight in shining armor, even as I denounced it to other singles and single parents. But finally, God helped me to really see it. It was almost like losing a friend when I lost the dream of that perfect someday. I cried. For months I was so sad because I finally came to the conclusion that there was no one who was going to come in and fix things for me. No man would make me complete and no relationship would bandage my aches and pains. Oh, how I longed for that. I didn't even know how much until I realized that it could never be.

God met me there. It was in that place of utter hopelessness that God brought me to His heart. I began calling out to Him in utter desperation. If no man was ever going to fulfill me, then I wanted God. That's where He had to take me. God had to expose this hidden little girl who believed her knight in shining armor may have gotten sidetracked but was still on his way. He had to take this little girl's heart and wrap His big strong arms around it and comfort me. Because it hurt beyond words. I wanted someone to make it okay. Someone, somewhere down the line, to make my life complete. And God said, *That's not how it works. I make you complete, and then your longing for companionship will be of Me, and you won't expect the world of your husband, and it will actually work.*

Okay, I said. And cried.

That's what it boils down to. God first. Relationship second. Over time I began to understand the greatest commandment. Love God with all your heart and love your neighbor as yourself (Matt. 22:37–39). I couldn't have ever loved a spouse when my desire for a husband was first in my life. That man would have let me down. I would have (and did) let people into my life whom I shouldn't have let in. Loving God first frees me to love others well and, best of all, frees me from the desperation that would have me settle for less than God's best.

So, now what?

God promises us through Psalm 37:4, "Delight yourself in the LORD and he will give you the desires of your heart." When He says that He will give us the desires of our heart, it is important that we understand what those desires are and whether they line up with His truth. According to Romans 3:23, all sin and fall short of the glory of God. So the perfect man who lives in our imagination doesn't exist. According to His Word, marriage is hard work. Don't get stuck just dreaming of the wedding day. Understand that relating to the same person under one roof for years and years can be very hard! Finally, we have to trust that God knows what He's doing. Impatience will drive us to make poor choices. Settle in, sink in, and delight in your heavenly Father. He has something for you. Not just in regard to your dating and future marriage relationship, but in keeping with His relationship with you.

Curious where you are in this journey? Answer the following questions and find out if your desires are on track or if they are in danger of blinding you.

Caution—it can be tempting to be less than truthful on quizzes like these. Don't do it! Be honest!

↬ When I meet a man who is interested in me:
A. I go out with him without giving much thought to what kind of guy he is.

B. As long as he's a decent guy, I'll give it a shot.

C. I have a few non-negotiables, including that he love God.

D. I have a long list of things that I'm looking for and I won't settle for anything less!

❧ I desire the man I date to have the following physical attributes:
A. Anything will do.
B. I'm not very particular but hope for someone handsome.
C. I'd like him to be reasonably fit and handsome.
D. I want muscles, the chiseled face . . . I want it all.

❧ When I think of how I will spend my time in a dating relationship:
A. I think about how good it will be to have someone there.
B. I imagine hanging out and watching movies, doing stuff together.
C. I envision good conversations, romantic evenings.
D. I dream of spending all our time together. I imagine flowers, romance, intimate evenings.

❧ When I think of my wedding day, I desire:
A. Wedding day? I just want to be with someone!
B. A justice of the peace is fine with me.
C. I hope to have a nice ceremony but I understand that it's not a point of arrival.
D. I have it all mapped out in my mind—it's going to be perfect!

❧ When I think of my marriage, I desire:
A. Marriage? I just want to be with someone!

B. Marriage is going to be great, a piece of cake.

C. Marriage will be wonderful, but it's going to take a lot of work.

D. My marriage is going to be perfect. My husband will take care of me, I'll take care of him, and we'll live happily ever after.

❧ When I think of waiting patiently for God's best, I think:

A. A day is too long.

B. A few months is my limit.

C. If God wants me to wait for a few years, I trust that He knows best.

D. I'll wait . . . until I say it's time.

❧ The true desire of my heart is:

A. To be loved.

B. To meet someone who loves me and wants to get married.

C. To meet a godly man, marry, and do life together with God.

D. To meet my prince charming who will whisk me off into the sunset.

Look over your answers and read the appropriate paragraph below.

The majority of your answers are A—Oh, how you yearn to know love! I understand that completely. But there is danger in that. You are setting yourself up to make a terrible mistake. The desire of your heart is one based in desperation. God has so much more for you! I would strongly encourage you to go through some counseling and find out what lies behind the need in your life. You are aching to be wanted and needed . . . please know that there is One who wants you, who loves you, *perfectly*. Go to Him first; pull out all the stops in pursuit of Him. Check out the next chapter for some tips on that. But whatever you do, wait on getting into a relationship with a man. Now is not the time.

The majority of your answers are B—Slow down. Take a little time before moving ahead in your relationship. You may not be thinking things through completely. There is more to a relationship then hanging out and loving each other. Understanding that will keep you from settling for someone who may be less than God's best.

The majority of your answers are C—You're on the right track. You have a good grasp on your desires and they seem realistic. Keep your heart tucked under the hand of your heavenly Father and move forward with a smile!

The majority of your answers are D—Chances are you are going to be disappointed. No man, date, or marriage can live up to the desire and expectation you are clinging to. It would be a good idea for you to have a heart-to-heart talk with some married friends to learn the truth about lifelong companionship. You might have to cry over some of those lost dreams, but don't worry; God will meet you there. Remember (or learn for the first time) that God is faithful, loving, and compassionate—so many of the very things you long for! After you settle into Him, He can give you real relationship, with all its ups and downs, highs and lows, tossed in together.

Chapter Two

Your First Love

Ever been in love? I'm thinking of that initial stage of total devotion, that place where we have all fallen with big smiles, butterflies, and pounding hearts. It is the period of bluer skies, vibrant colors, and joyful expectations. It's positively the best feeling around. Do you remember what it felt like to share that love with a friend? "I love him," we've said. "He's amazing! He's kind and funny and handsome and intelligent and charming . . ." On and on and on we go. I've said it myself and I've heard it from women all around me. Colored glasses tinted our favorite shade. He can do no wrong, and heaven lies within reach.

I used to love talking about my current beau. Whoever he was at the time received glowing reviews to all who would listen. It almost felt like talking about him brought him closer to me.

Unfortunately, the feeling never lasted. He would turn out to be not so charming or not very kind or not nearly as wonderful as I'd once believed. And of course, it was always unfortunate to discover that *I* wasn't the epitome of perfection either.

But God *is* perfection. And I've fallen in love with Him. He *is* that someone who is charming and kind and compassionate and wonderful and romantic. I find myself bragging about Him to anyone who will listen. He has filled this place in me and brought me joy unlike anything I've ever known. He really does make the sky bluer and colors more vibrant and joy more real. I can be having the worst day and He will show up through the hug of a friend, a smile, a rose, a song. He is ever faithful and always tender. He is absolutely out for my best. He'll never leave me nor forsake me, and He gave His life to have a relationship with me. He sought me out in my darkest places when I had absolutely no reason to hope, and He loved me there. He gave me a future.

And so I fell in love. Not in the way I fell for men. That was usually a quick thing that dissipated as reality set in. My falling in love with Jesus has happened in the opposite way. Beginning with skepticism, it has deepened and broadened as reality has set in. The more I get to know Him, the more I fall in love with Him. And I have a sneaking suspicion it will only go deeper from here.

Well, Elsa, you may be saying to yourself, *that's fine for you. But what about me? You haven't done the things I've done. You don't know how God sees me.* Oh, but I do. It's written all throughout His Word. Sam Storms, author of *A Singing God*, puts it perfectly as he talks about Psalm 103. In that Psalm, David shared the depth of God's love and passion for us. He said in verse 14 that God knows how we are formed, He remembers that we are dust.

Don't miss that little word "for" that opens verse 14. What a stunning little word. It's only one word, but it will turn your entire grasp on who God is and how He relates to you upside down. My earthly mind tells me that it is precisely because God knows my frame that He would want nothing to do with me. Intimate and uncomfortably specific insight into the sinful propensity of our souls is the very thing we think would make it impossible for God to feel anything but revulsion when He looks at us. But the psalmist says it is because God has such knowledge that He chooses not to reward us according to our iniquities, but rather to shower us with loving-kindness, compassion, and forgiveness.

You are dust, I am dust. We are all frail, forgetful, ungrateful, weak, finite creatures, formed from the dust of the earth. Worse still, when we mix in the reality of sin, our dust turns to mud. God knows it all, and for that reason shows loving-kindness beyond measure and mercy forever.
—Sam Storms, The Singing God

Storms goes on to say that when we see and experience that kind of love, it moves us into greater commitment. We stand in awe of it, we long for more, and we want to eliminate anything that would get in the way of our experiencing it to its fullest. So how do we come to see and understand love of that magnitude? How do we sink ourselves so deeply into Jesus that He becomes our first love, the one we brag about and long for? Here are a few tools that may help you on the journey.

Get to Know Him

Imagine you are looking to find that special someone. You pick up the Sunday paper and catch sight of the personal ads. Which one of these would capture your eye?

Dictator looking for subjects. Don't care about needs, hopes, and dreams. Looking for someone who will follow my orders, keep their eyes to the ground, and walk twenty paces behind me. Will provide rules and regulations. Nothing more.

Bully looking to condemn and reject. I have a perpetually wagging finger that will live in your face. You will never do anything good enough for me, no matter how hard you may try. I'm forever right, you are forever wrong, and you'll have to get used to it. Call me.

Loving Savior seeking lost love. Willing to carry the daily burdens of life, infinitely interested in hurts and sorrows, longing to reveal precious future to beloved. Will give up life to know you, will guide you in paths laden with blessings. Will support and protect when life seems too much.

Which one of these ads describes the God you see in your mind? What do you believe about God? If you see Him as the dictator, the condemner, the one who is forever angry . . . why would you want to spend time with Him? Why would you want to ask Him to be your first love, your top priority? What would draw your heart to a God of such harsh character?

How you view God will greatly determine your desire for Him. *Get to know Him.* His character and His promises are everywhere in the Bible. His heart of love and compassion is revealed over and over again. He reveals how much He loves the broken, has compassion on the rebellious, seeks out the lonely. Read about the Israelites in the Old Testament. What a story of love! God kept coming back for His people no matter how far they had gone astray; His merciful touch understood exactly where each of His children were and met them there. In the New Testament, the power of His grace and touch transformed lives. He loved broken people throughout Scripture! These are the character traits of our God! He is a good God who wants to connect personally with you. And unless you believe that, He will never become your top priority, the love of your life.

The first step to putting God in that top spot is getting to know Him. "Taste and see that the LORD is good," says Psalm 34:8.

Spend Time with Him

I never would have imagined it. There I was, on a Friday night, with nothing but hours stretched out before me. I was sitting in front of the fireplace at a small bed & breakfast, and I was on a date. With my heavenly Father. Years earlier I would have laughed at someone spending time with God in that way. The thought of two days spent in His company would have been completely foreign to me.

Yet there I was . . . and there was no place I would have rather been. I read through some Scripture, journaled, cried. I could feel Him there with me; I could see Him in the flickering flames, in the magnificent sunset outside my windows. I could even, as I lay my head on the bed that night, feel His gentle tenderness and His heart of love toward me. It was amazing. It was romantic. And I was astounded. Over the years of calling out to Him, something had happened. He had become my everything.

Through my journaling and Scripture reading, I felt Him direct my heart toward something He was trying to tell me. The songs I listened to seemed to direct me to the same things. He used the time to communicate with me, and my faith deepened.

All of us have different ways in which we feel most comfortable connecting to God. Some of us are moved beyond expression when we encounter beauty in nature. Others of us fall in love with Him when we hear a beautiful song or see a drama. Others of us journal our way to His heart. While all of us can and *must* connect to Him through Scripture, there are different things that draw the very heart of who we are. What is that heart connection for you? Is it music? Writing? Books? Whatever it is that draws us closer, that is the very thing we need to incorporate into our lives as a non-negotiable.

Often we will learn a lot about God without ever encountering who He is. We need to find out what moves us to our core. What is it that makes us yearn for Him? Knowing about God will do nothing to settle the longing for true love that we have. Experiencing Him through word, song, or beauty transforms us at the deepest place. And then we will be far more hesitant to let Him go. We will give it our all even when our heart becomes impatient and strong arms come to woo us away. Where's your heart, ladies? Does it swoon for the One who loves you most? If not, maybe it's time to spend some time with your true knight in shining armor.

Begin with some time every morning, steal away an afternoon, go away for a night. Start simple. It doesn't have to look any particular way; just take your Bible, some books, some music, and a journal and ask Him to meet with you. He's been waiting for this time; you can count on Him to be there! As you take that time and He meets you, your love and understanding of Him will grow. You will get to know the heart of who He is . . . a God who is in love with you!

Hang Out with His People

It's hard to grow closer to God in a vacuum. Setting yourself into the right environments is tremendously important. If you are not attending a church, take that first step. Commit to attending regularly. If you are attending a church, take the next step by getting involved in a small group. Build relationships and friendships with people who love God and watch how He shows Himself through them. Hebrews 10:25 says, "Let us not give up meeting together, as some are in the habit of doing."

Ask Him

There have been many moments when I've wanted anything but God. I've wanted the touch of another human, a cigarette, several hours of dreamless sleep, chocolate cake. But the last thing I wanted was to come to the Perfect One as the imperfect mess I was. So I asked: "Create in me a desire for You!" He answered! He is faithful. Sometimes we just heap condemnation on condemnation, thinking how horrible we are that we simply don't feel like connecting to God. Yet prophets and believers of old dealt with the same condition. "Create in me a pure heart," cried David (Psalm 51:10). Or the Israelites—they were making idols and calling out to other gods *even as the one true God provided for their every need!* Our humanity, this terrible habit of getting stuck in other things, has been a shared frustration among all of us throughout history. For all have sinned and fall short—nobody ever gets it completely right (Rom. 3:23).

We can come to our Father and set that before Him. He loves the truth. "Lord, I want to want You. I want to fall in love with You but don't even know where to begin. I keep getting stuck. I mess up and don't want to come to You. Or I expect [insert boyfriend's name here] to meet my needs, and then I get mad at him and feel sorry for myself and forget all about the fact that *You* are the one I can trust to take care of me. Please help me."

We are promised in Matthew 7:7, "Ask and it will be given to you; seek and you will find; knock and the door will be opened to you. For everyone who asks receives; he who seeks finds; and to him who knocks the door will be opened."

Ask God to draw you near.

Abide in Him

Imagine that you have experienced a taste of God's love; you've asked, you've sought, and you've spent the time. Everything should be set, right? I have in my memory many moments when I have encountered God. Sometimes I am tempted to live off those memories without creating time for fresh ones. John 15 goes into detail about the importance of abiding continually in Christ. "I am the vine; you are the branches. If a man remains in me and I in him, he will bear much fruit; apart from me you can do nothing. . . . If you remain in me and my words remain in you, ask whatever you wish, and it will be given you. . . . As the Father has loved me, so have I loved you. Now remain in my love" (John 15:5, 7, 9).

Abide in Him. It's a continual process that needs our attention!

Keep Him There

Elaine was single. She was growing in God and had been searching for His love. She began engaging in a daily quiet time, participating in a small group, building friendships, and attending church. She was doing all the right things.

When Bill came into the picture, Elaine was at first very resistant. She knew that she had to get some things straight before she started dating. She tried to avoid his attention but found herself thinking about him more and more often. Within just a few months, she started dating Bill and walked away from her pursuit of God. It wasn't that she meant for it to happen, in fact she even felt a little guilty about the whole thing. It was just that her time was precious, and Bill wasn't really interested in going to church . . . and his arms felt real. She decided in her heart that it would be okay. She'd invest in her relationship with Bill now and go back to the God thing later.

How many times has this happened? All the time. I've done it to God myself, and I've seen women and men do it over and over. They break off a relationship, come to God, start getting more involved, meet someone else, and off they go. God becomes the ultimate rebound man, dumped as soon as real arms come calling.

I share this without condemnation. After all, God is very familiar with our every weakness and loves us deeply. Yet there has to be a way to avoid this cycle. A huge part of it is understanding where our true value comes from. Many times we're swayed from God because someone has made us feel good about ourselves. They make us feel beautiful, or important, or treasured. Dr. Don Raunikar puts it this way in *Choosing God's Best*: "We're all searching for what makes our lives count—for the person or the something that will keep us from feeling worthless. Far too many of us base our personal worth on what we believe the most important people in our lives think about us. We're constantly looking to someone else just to be told we are significant."

Great, we think. Yup, that's me. When I hear a real voice telling me I'm precious, I run to that voice. But what do I *do* about it? There are a few things that I believe will help to keep you on track, even when real arms are pulling you away from your first love.

Remind yourself of the truth. Plaster the truth everywhere. I'm talking about the Scriptures that speak of your value, the treasure you are to Christ. For if you believe that, truly believe it deep down inside, there will be nothing that will take you from Him. No man will be able to distract you because your identity and your love will be secure. You will be able to decide in your heart that the practices we discussed in this chapter (knowing, asking, seeking, abiding) are non-negotiables, because without them, we are quickly deceived. With your identity firmly in place and your value in Him, you will be able to move forward in wisdom. You will be able to walk into a dating relationship, knowing that your value has nothing to do with your date and certain that your first love will remain first.

Covenant with a friend. Accountability and community will be a theme throughout this book. We will discuss the importance of friendship in dating in Chapter Four. For now, understand the importance of having a friend who will ask you the hard questions. Commit to them that even if you begin dating, you will stay engaged with God. No matter what.

Stay involved in community. Don't sacrifice your small group or friendship time to be with your date. Make these items non-negotiable in your life. A godly man will not only honor that, he will be doing the same thing himself. If the man you want to date is not a believer, don't even go there. Please. We'll discuss the reasons why in a later chapter. For now, trust me!

Serve others. When we are serving others actively, it will be much more difficult for the dating process to distract us in an unhealthy way. There are several reasons for that. We'll be getting connection with others, so we won't be as desperate for love. We'll discover the joy of meeting the real needs of people, and that will build our confidence and security. We will have commitments (every Wednesday we help with the women's ministry, every Sunday we set out bulletins) that will keep us coming to church even when we might be tempted to miss. And we will be doing exactly what God commands us to do . . . loving each other. We'll be in His will, and when we are in that place, we'll be very hesitant to leave.

Have dates with God. If we look at our relationship with God as an obligation of time and service, we won't be very interested in staying close. If, however, we are creating times of intimacy, we'll continue the process of falling in love.

Be real with Him. Every one of us experiences unhealthy distraction from time to time. And we may have the best strategy in the world to remain connected and suddenly find ourselves missing Him. Tell Him. I can't tell you how many times I've come to the Father and said, "I'm thinking about this guy again. Way more than I should. I don't want to, I wish I wasn't, but I'm yearning in a way that I'm just not happy about! Will You please help me? I know You know me. I'm a hopeless romantic and I know that's one of the things that You love about me . . . but please help!" And He does. He really does.

Rather than hide your feelings from the One who created you and hope He doesn't notice that you've been dreaming about what's-his-name 24/7, just be honest. He will absolutely meet you in that place. "There is no condemnation in Christ Jesus." All of our thoughts and feelings are important to the One who created us, even when they are pulling us away, *especially* when they are pulling us away from Him. Be real with God. He already knows what you're up to anyway!

A Thought . . .

All of these tools will help to keep us connected with God as we get into dating relationships. Please understand that thinking about a man is not a bad thing. Getting warm fuzzies about a potential dating relationship is completely natural. Wondering about your time together, what he might be doing, all of these things are as God designed. Yet we, as women, don't typically stop there. Relationships with men have a tendency to take up a big part of our thought life. The above tools will help keep your Father first.

Where are you in your relationship with God? Is He first? Is your value set firmly in Him? Are you in danger of abandoning Him? Answer these questions to see where you might be.

✎ I see God as:
A. An angry God. I'm afraid He is frustrated with me most of the time.
B. A loving God, as long as I follow the rules.
C. A good God who cares about my decisions and me.
D. A big warm fuzzy in the sky; He loves everyone and doesn't really care about the particulars.

✎ I believe that God is:
A. Mean and unforgiving.
B. A taskmaster, hard to please.
C. A loving Father, a merciful Companion, and a Holy Lord.
D. A loving God, accepting of everything and anything.

✎ Spending time with God (quiet time):
A. I have a hard time spending any time with God.
B. I have a quiet time here and there and feel guilty for not taking more time.
C. I enjoy my time with God; something is missing when I don't get it.
D. God is everywhere; I don't feel like I have to take specific time with Him.

✎ I am involved in my church community in these ways:
A. I am not involved.

B. I go to church on Sundays. I never miss, but I don't necessarily engage.

C. I'm involved in church and also attend a small group.

D. I get there when it's convenient. I figure God is happy when I show up.

❧ I serve my church in these ways:

A. I don't serve in any capacity.

B. I serve as much as I can. I figure if I serve enough, God will bring someone good into my life.

C. I am committed to serve several times a month.

D. I sometimes volunteer for things, if it sounds like it might be fun.

❧ When I think of reading the Bible:

A. I dread it. I don't understand it and don't like to read it.

B. I read it religiously, but it doesn't seem to impact my life.

C. I take the words personally, memorizing them and applying them to my own circumstances.

D. I read the good parts—about love and hope and kindness. Sometimes.

❧ When I start dating someone:

A. God is the first thing to go.

B. I tend to hide from God because I never seem to get it right.

C. I bring all my feelings to God and He helps me sort them out.

D. God is love. I figure He's happy if I'm happy.

☙ **In my dating history:**
A. God has never been involved.
B. God was involved but usually only because I felt guilty.
C. I've kept God first in my relationships.
D. God has been my rebound man. I'm always more committed when I'm not dating someone.

☙ **When God thinks of me:**
A. He is typically disappointed.
B. He has a scorecard and keeps close track of my mistakes. He is often frustrated that I don't do better.
C. God loves me deeply and passionately, just as I am. He also loves me enough to grow me to maturity through my circumstances.
D. God loves me. God loves everyone.

☙ **When I think of falling in love with God, of making Him my first love:**
A. It seems like an impossibility.
B. When I'm doing well, I feel good about our relationship. When I make mistakes, I wonder if He will leave. I don't feel secure enough to fall in love.
C. The more I get to know about Him, the more I fall for Him. Our relationship is growing.
D. It's never been that intimate; He's just there. I love Him, but it's not a deep thing.

Look over your answers and read the appropriate paragraph below.

The majority of your answers are A—My friend, you are in danger. The God that you think is real is not. He is not an angry God whom you cannot please. He is loving, compassionate, tender, merciful, kind, and gracious. He thinks of you with love and even knows the number of hairs on your head. Please take the time to get to know your true heavenly Father. Don't date yet. Get to know Him first. Otherwise you will find yourself in a relationship that cannot feed the hunger in your soul. Call out to God, get involved in a church, find a place where you can experience Him, and dig in. He is waiting for you with outstretched arms!

The majority of your answers are B—You tend to see God as a taskmaster, someone who only wants you if you are squeaky-clean and doing all the right things. It's easy to abandon a God like that if someone comes along and loves you in your messes. God loves you in your messes! Of course He longs to protect our hearts and gives us rules to help us draw near to Him, but He is not based in rules. You are loved with an everlasting love that comes from who He is, not who you are. I would encourage you to take some romantic time with God. What stirs your heart of love for Him? Spend some more time in those things: reading the Bible regularly, listening to music, observing nature, reading good books that describe His love. You will be glad you did!

The majority of your answers are C—You have a good understanding of God, His love, and His plan for relationship with you. Continue to use the tools in this chapter to stay connected to His heart. And take some time to teach others what you have learned; there are many who need you!

The majority of your answers are D—I'm glad that you see God as loving and kind. That's a good thing and a big first step to developing real and vital relationship. What you need to do at this point is take a look at His character. He has more for you. He is a very specific God with a very specific plan for each one of us. He is also holy and righteous and has set certain guidelines in place to help draw us near to the heart of Him. Please take some time to study His plans and purposes, set throughout His Word.

Chapter Three

Your Story

Karen grew up with a father whose emotions controlled the household. When he was angry, the children cowered in fear. When he was frustrated, they were to blame. Little they did placated his temper, no matter how hard they tried. "I remember one occasion," Karen said quietly, "when I was in elementary school. My dad was drinking hot coffee at the kitchen table while we were eating breakfast. Our table was one of those metal tables with the leaves that come up. He put his elbow on the table leaf while holding his coffee. The leaf dropped down and the coffee spilled all over me. He yelled at me and claimed it was my fault. All I can remember is cowering from his anger and being afraid to cry."

As Karen grew into adulthood, her father continued to manipulate, blame, and control through his expressions of anger or his bouts of stormy silence. When Karen was old enough to make her own choices, she ran into the arms of another man. There was only one problem. He was exactly like her dad. "He was just like my father," Karen said, "so much so that on one occasion I was at a meeting and sat between them. During the meeting, Dad leaned over and whispered something to me and sat up. A moment later Joe leaned over and whispered the exact same words to me. They were both very controlling men and I let them control me.

"For fifteen years we did what Joe wanted, when Joe wanted, how Joe wanted. My opinion did not matter and that destroyed what little self-esteem I had. I was afraid that Joe would leave me if I didn't do what he wanted. I am not the prettiest woman and he is a very good-looking man. I felt lucky that he supposedly fell in love with me. Now looking back, I know that he loved the way he could control me. He loved the things that I did for him. He did not abuse me physically, but he certainly did emotionally and mentally. We were together from the time I was 28 until I was 43. My biggest sadness comes when I think about the children that I will never have. He never wanted any, and now it's too late for me."

Karen's childhood had a significant impact on her future choices. Once she was out of her father's grip, she didn't look back for a moment. If she had, she may have saved herself fifteen years of heartache. For some of us, it seems easier to leave our past far behind us. We feel as though we have already lived through it, and that was a huge accomplishment in itself. The thought of revisiting our childhood seems like a waste of time. Not to mention that the energy it would take to rehash old hurts and pain could leave us frozen in fear or running for the hills.

Why Dig Around in Our Past?

Because our stories define our choices. Our stories

are a part of who we are. The circumstances and people that influenced us have a tremendous impact on the way we live our lives now. If we refuse to acknowledge that, to dig a little deeper and discover the things that have molded us, we end up living with habits and under a certain set of beliefs that just aren't true. Such beliefs will have a tremendous influence on our dating future. Think of Karen's story. She thought her father's treatment defined her as a bad child. She was not bad. She was a sweet girl caught in a bad place. Yet since she started to believe that there was something wrong with her, that she was unworthy of love and affection, she grew up to be a woman who believed she was unworthy of love and affection. She determined in that quiet place inside that she would never receive more than the anger and disappointment her father poured into her and she chose a man who gave her exactly that.

Brent Curtis and John Eldredge could have been talking about Karen when they shared this thought in their book, *The Sacred Romance*: "When we live with so little love, we will grasp onto what we do receive in a way that becomes defining. These moments may not reveal our true identity and calling, but they're all we've got."

Then there's Jane. Her father was cold and distant throughout her early years. No matter what she did, there was little response on his part. So when Jane first encountered boys outside of her family, she found a whole new realm of opportunities for love. She didn't care what type of boys they were. If they liked her or if they gave her attention, she liked them. The word *choice* never even entered her mind. The only qualification she required of the next boyfriend was that he love her. His character, his likes, his pet peeves—none of that mattered. As long as he loved her, she responded.

Jane needed to discover her own story. She needed to understand her father's role in her choices so that she could move forward to forgive, grow, and heal. She would never know real relationship without those steps—just the counterfeit ones that come when hunger outweighs the truth.

Our stories define our expectations. Angie was an only child, doted on by her older parents. The sun rose and set on their little girl's life, and they revolved their own schedules around her wants and needs. Angie grew up with the sense that she deserved an excessive amount of attention. When she started dating Anthony, he gave her that attention. Flowers, romantic dates, sweet love notes. Angie knew that she found the one for her. Yet as time wore on, Anthony settled back into his work schedule and Angie started feeling abandoned. She began to demand more and more of Anthony's time, devotion, and interest. Anthony began pulling further and further away. While he loved Angie, he couldn't do all the things she asked of him. He began to feel frustrated and, ultimately, he left the relationship.

Each of us has a certain expectation for romance, dating, and marriage. We expect a certain amount of time together, a certain level of care, a particular type of gift, card, kiss, or expression of love. If we grew up in an environment where there was no fighting, a single conflict might crumble us. If we grew up in a home where fighting with each other meant love, we might quickly alienate a new partner.

Understanding our expectations is another reason to dig into our history. God defines love in a certain way, and

He characterizes the giving and receiving of love very specifically. That means that we need to bring all of our expectations, our story, our history under His truth and examine it carefully there. Did we learn that love was patient and kind? Did our parents live out the truth that genuine love is not jealous or envious? That it doesn't delight in evil, but celebrates truth? If we examine our story in light of God's truth, He will show us what is faulty and teach us a new way.

Our past story might be robbing us of a future. It's easy to say that we need to deal with our past, but many of us still don't want to go there. *Well*, we think to ourselves, *it was horrible when that one thing happened, but when you compare it to what other people have been through, it really doesn't amount to much.* Or others may say, *When I start looking into my past, I feel like my life is a black hole, and if I step to the edge I'll be sucked into the pain. I'm afraid if I start looking I will never stop, and it will destroy me. I'll spend the rest of my life dealing with stuff that's better left buried right where it is.*

In addition, many of us have built a handy set of defenses. They may be frustrating—the addictions, the men, the isolation—but we know them and they're comfortable. The thought of giving them up in pursuit of this fuzzy picture of health bucks against everything inside of us. Especially if that noble pursuit doesn't necessarily have a clearly defined end.

Yet there is something, something inside of us, that yearns for more, that knows and believes there is more to life than what we've experienced. We know that love can be joyful, that romance can be fun, and that God designed relationships as a rich blessing . . . and we want that. We also know in that quiet place, where we are truthful with ourselves, that we can't have those relationships unless we battle the lies that keep us in their grip. Don't let your past rob your future!

Here are some others who share the same sentiment:

It is imperative that you take steps of healing. If the spirits of anger, bitterness, revenge, self-pity, and fear have attached themselves to your life, you will inevitably attract a person with similar spiritual problems.
—P.B. Wilson, *Knight in Shining Armor*

Marriage does not change our past. It works in just the opposite way. It tends to reveal past hurts, and all our efforts to keep those memories hidden may eventually result in a crumbling marriage.
—Don Raunikar, *Choosing God's Best*

Broken women find it difficult to maintain relationships. They are always looking for someone who can carry the weight of their pain. The only man I know who is attracted to carrying others' pain is Jesus.
—T.D. Jakes, *The Lady, Her Lover, and Her Lord*

If you hold to my teaching, you are really my disciples. Then you will know the truth, and the truth will set you free. —Jesus, John 8:31–32

There's the key. The truth will set us free. We don't have to make choices based on the holes left by others. We can decide whether a man fits our standards before we move forward, without feeling obligated to return his love.

We don't have to race into a relationship for fear we will never know connection. Imagine what it would be like to be grounded and secure in who we are in Christ. Imagine if we knew what our weaknesses were and were able to immediately apply God's truth. Imagine what it would feel like to date on His terms, to be confident and secure in our choices. That freedom awaits us and it is absolutely worth it.

How Do We Unlock Our Story?

Some of us may think that we don't have much in our past to work through. Perhaps you were one of the lucky ones who grew up in a loving and secure environment. That's wonderful! Celebrate! But still take the time to look in the corners. Each one of us, no matter what our story, can find tremendous benefit in seeing where our values, expectations, and pain come from. None of us make it through life without our share of scars, and God longs to heal each one.

There are several different ways to understand who we are and why we make the romantic and life choices that we do.

Recovery groups. Let's go back to Karen. She took the time to see the pattern of hurt that her father initiated in her life. She took her broken heart to her Father in heaven and asked that He show her the hurtful patterns in her life. One of the ways she did that was to attend her church's recovery group. They dealt with different materials, including *Making Peace with Your Past* by Tim Sledge, *Breaking Free* by Beth Moore, and *Moving Beyond Your Past*, also by Tim Sledge. These groups met in a large group for the first half hour and then broke off into smaller groups for discussion.

Recovery groups are a great tool for exposing painful issues from our past. The group environment is also wonderful in that it helps connect us in community and reminds us that we are not alone in our struggles to understand. Your home church may not offer such groups, but if you investigate around your area, you may find other churches that do offer them. Recovery groups are a great first step in understanding our stories and our choices.

Counseling. I looked at my counselor with wide eyes, my heart pounding in my ears. She had just told me that she *understood*. She understood why I felt lost and alone, she agreed that things that happened to me were not fair or good. She affirmed my hurt, and with tenderness she let me cry. With godly wisdom she walked me through things that I couldn't see, exposed unforgiveness, and revealed hurt. I cried almost the whole time, but it helped. Tremendously. For me, I just needed to know that I wasn't defective, that the circumstances around me were hard for a young girl to face and understand. She relieved me of the sense that I was somehow broken and a burden to those around me. She helped to free me from my past.

A godly counselor is an invaluable tool in navigating our life stories. Sometimes it's very difficult for us to see objectively. There is absolutely no shame in asking for help. The wise walk with the wise (Prov. 13:20). It takes courage and strength to recognize that we can't see or do it all on our own. If this is the course for you, I encourage you to take that step now. And please don't let finances keep you from getting this help. Often we use lack of money as an excuse. Instead, pray about it. Ask your church community where you might find someone who would be willing to help. Investigate.

Run to your Father. God is infinitely interested in us, in our hurts, in our growth. He wants us to find our source of strength in Him so that we can love others out of the wealth of love He has poured into us. When we are firmly set into our Father's hand, we can love freely, generously, and with wisdom. The greatest thing we can do in this process is ask God to reveal the portions of our life that need to be addressed.

Doing personal work is wonderful, but it's imperative that we do it under the guidance of the Holy Spirit. It's the difference between peeling an onion layer by layer and cutting through to the very core. The Holy Spirit is gentle in healing us. He will take us, as we are ready, to the different places that need our attention. I know that seems hard to define; how do we allow the Holy Spirit to show us? Ask Him. Before you use any of the above tools, ask Him to direct their use in your life. God is faithful; He will not ignore your cry to grow in understanding and wisdom. Remember His character: "Yet the LORD longs to be gracious to you; he rises to show you compassion" (Isa. 30:18). He is in pursuit of our hearts and is more than willing to clear out the clutter so that we can see Him clearly.

We [those who minister to broken hearts] *see grown women running to the altar, but the Father hears the sound of the pitter-patter of little feet. They are running to the altar. There is nowhere left to run. These are broken little girls grown taller but still bent over. They are filled with regret and secrets, scars and traumas. They have run from arm to arm, from man to man. They have run until they were tired*

of seeing the same things happen over and over again. To run without direction is like running rapidly in a circle. You spend a lot of energy, but you have so few results. . . . Have you ever looked back over your life and felt as though you have exhausted yourself traveling, but you still have not reached your destination?
—T.D. Jakes, *The Lady, Her Lover, and Her Lord*

Ask the Father, take the steps, understand your motives and needs in regard to relationship. That is the only way we will keep from making the same mistakes over and over.

How Long Does It Take?

Ultimately, understanding our past in a way that builds our future is a lifelong process. God will always take the time to reveal to us the next layer, to heal the places just below the surface. As with everything else, there is no "point of arrival" where all is well with the world forever and ever. Yet a core understanding *is* needed before we can be good and godly partners in a love relationship.

The core understanding? I wish I could say that it takes a couple of weeks, a few months, a year. Each person is different. If the wounds are deep, they will need some lengthy exploration and healing time. That may make us hesitate to even go there. But cling to this thought: Continuing as we are will rob us of many blessings in our future. It's not going to get better on its own, which means a whole lot more years of painful relationships and heartache. Yet a few years of hard work can bring about tremendous change and, ultimately, boatloads of joy! It's so worth it. Plunge in!

For others of us, it may only take a few months, or for those who were raised in the ultimate godly environment, it may be even shorter. If possible, this kind of work is best done while alone, because we tend to grow through it into different people. In addition, at the other end of our labors we may long for a different type of companion then we did at the start. If you are already in a relationship, perhaps it is something the two of you can commit to. Promise each other that you will address these things in your pasts so that your future has a chance.

Now What?

Let's say that we've done the work, we've walked through our story, and the wounds have been healed. Now we can throw ourselves headlong into the next relationship that comes along, right? Wrong! Sorry . . . for you see, God can heal the broken places, but we may still have a propensity toward a certain type of behavior . . . especially if we've been living a certain way for a long time. We need to understand what our weaknesses are and then actively protect ourselves from them. Think of it—what good does it do if we say to ourselves, *Hmmm, this isn't the guy for me*, and then go for it anyway? Awareness does not mean that we will have a handle on our first impulses. I'm certain that's why God promises that His power is made perfect in weakness (2 Cor. 12:9). Once we are aware and we run to Him, *He* empowers us to make different choices. But we have to cling to Him! Trust me! I've learned this the hard way. Here are a couple of thoughts that may help you to be successful in your decision making.

How to Protect Yourself—The Forest and the Water

I was driving home from visiting a friend one morning when I saw the most amazing tree. It was set in the middle of a field and lacked any kind of protection from the wind. Because of its vulnerability, it was bent nearly horizontal to the ground by the steady pressure of the wind against its trunk. Immediately I saw us in that tree. Perhaps for years you have experienced a steady wind of whispers. Whispers that say, "You're not worthy . . . No one is ever going to love you . . . You're a mess . . . You'll never get it right." Maybe those whispers were conveyed through looks, poor grades, mean classmates, or broken relationships. Maybe they were whispered through your own thought life and you began to steadily bend through the enduring pressure. You are still a tree. You are still a child of God. Yet maybe all you can see is the ground right there in front of you. Perhaps you've been bent so far that you don't believe you are worthy to fully experience the storms or the sunshine of real relationship.

Imagine, in your mind's eye, our Lord. He can transplant the tree into a forest. There, He can set us beside a stream of living water and place us underneath the cover of the tall, strong trees around us. He can protect us from the wind there. He can attach us to the limbs of the steady trees beside us, pulling us upward with a steady pressure. With whispers of love and truth and hope, He will draw our bent trunk skyward. He won't force us in one quick jerk to stand tall, for He knows we may break. So it is that over time we can grow as we were meant to grow, standing taller and taller, experiencing all of life, love, and relationship. It is then that we can know both the storms and the sunshine, and still stand strong.

The forest. You have to surround yourself with people who love God and love you. Let them be your forest. Let them pull you skyward and show you how you were meant to grow. We need to ask the strong trees in our life to tell us the truth. We need to let them into our hearts and our lives so that they can help us if we start making the same poor choices. They can remind us that so-and-so is a lot like our father, or that what's-his-name is very reminiscent of the last what's-his-name that broke our heart a year ago. We are meant to live in community, and we desperately need one another to do this well. We'll be discussing more of this in our next chapter.

The wind and the water. It is so important that we replace the steady whispers that are invading our thought life and remind ourselves of the truth. We need to sink our roots into the living water of God's Word. We must do whatever we have to do, whether we write Scripture on the palm of our hand, write it on note cards, or memorize it. God's truth is the sword by which we fight the lies that sneak in when we least expect it. His Word is our strength, our hope, the fiery dart we throw at the enemy. Are you familiar with any of these relational whispers? "You will always be alone," our enemy says. "Joe Shmoe is the only one who loves you. You better hold on to that one. So he doesn't have everything you hoped for—give the guy a break. At least he loves you." Or, "Do you realize you're the only one home alone tonight? What a loser . . . what's wrong with you? Better go out and find someone soon. There's that bar downtown, what could it hurt?"

That's when you pull out God's Word:

Never will I leave you; never will I forsake you.
—Hebrews 13:5

And I pray that you, being rooted and established in love, may have power, together with all the saints, to grasp how wide and long and high and deep is the love of Christ, and to know this love that surpasses knowledge—that you may be filled to the measure of all the fullness of God.
—Ephesians 3:17–19

I trust in God's unfailing love for ever and ever.
—Psalm 52:8

Every good and perfect gift is from above, coming down from the Father of the heavenly lights, who does not change like shifting shadows. —James 1:17

Whoever drinks the water I give him will never thirst. Indeed, the water I give him will become in him a spring of water welling up to eternal life. —John 4:14

The enemy and his lies will flee when we draw near to God through His Word. James 4:7 makes that promise: "Resist the devil, and he will flee from you." Come near to God and He will come near to you.

A Lot of Hard Work

So, we think to ourselves, *that's a lot of work!* First we have to figure out our story, then we have to know our weaknesses, and finally we have to keep reminding ourselves of the truth. It is hard work. But the payoff?

We will know when to run and who to run from. Remember Karen and the fifteen years she stayed with Joe? Don't lose fifteen years, my friends. Take the time to do the work now.

We will make better choices and attract different people. We tend to attract those who are dealing with matching issues. Without even realizing it, we give off a certain vibe that attracts similar people. If we take the time to get healthy by discovering our story, involving ourselves in community, and telling ourselves the truth, we will attract healthier people. No relationship can make us healthy. Only God, through the Holy Spirit, can bring about the healing we long for. And He will do it!

Every one of us can experience growth and healing. He promises in Ephesians that He is faithful to our completion. Not just the pastor types, not just the lady down the street who seems to get it right. But you and me. Ladies who have maybe stumbled here and there, who get ourselves distracted and sometimes lose focus. He is faithful to our completion. And He won't give up on us, ever.

The work is worth it, my friends. Get to a counselor; get involved in a group. Even if your "issues" seem minute. Every one of us could use a good, healthy perspective on what's taken place in our lives. The more we understand how our stories formed us and the more we set ourselves in places of growth and healing, the better decisions we will make in our future. And don't forget to let the Holy Spirit remain in the driver seat. He won't let you stay stuck for an eternity. He'll move you through at the right pace, and He'll keep you from getting too self-absorbed. When our healing is God-directed, it's no Band-Aid; it's a miracle.

Where are you on this journey? Is your story defining your choices in an unhealthy way? Do you need to take some healing time? Answer the following questions to see where you might be: (Remember to be honest!)

❧ My relationship with my father:
A. My father was never around.

B. My father was there, but he was cold, distant, and angry.

C. My father was a good guy; he just worked a lot.

D. My father was loving and supportive. He was involved in my life.

❧ My relationship with my mother:
A. My mother was never around.

B. My mother was there but didn't seem to care about me.

C. My mother was a wonderful lady, but we didn't have much time together.

D. My mother was nurturing and involved in my life.

❧ When I think of my childhood:
A. I don't think about my childhood; it was horrible.

B. It makes me sad; I missed out on a lot of things.

C. It was okay; we had our ups and downs.

D. I have good memories of my childhood.

❧ My parents were:
A. Divorced and bitter.

B. Divorced but civil.

C. Married and unhappy.

D. Happily married.

As I was growing up I felt:
A. Like nobody cared about me.
B. Like I was a burden.
C. That I was loved, but not really noticed.
D. Important to my parents and siblings.

When I think about myself as a human being:
A. I believe that I am worthless.
B. I tend to make a lot of mistakes and don't get many things right.
C. I'm an average woman; there is nothing especially impressive about me.
D. I was created on purpose and by design; I am valuable.

Most of my dating relationships:
A. Have been one mistake after another.
B. I continue to make poor choices, though I don't know why.
C. My relationships have been okay; I just want more.
D. Most of my relationships have been rich and rewarding, with a few mishaps along the way.

In general, when I am around other people:
A. I worry what they are thinking about me.
B. I don't typically fit in with other people.
C. I'm comfortable, but I only let people see what I want them to see.
D. I'm very comfortable in the company of others.

Look over your answers and read the appropriate paragraph below.

The majority of your answers are A— Friend, I don't think you know how deeply loved you are. You have walked through some difficult things and your wounds may be painful, but know this: your heavenly Father is faithful to your completion. I want to remind you of Isaiah 30:18—"He rises to show you compassion." Rises! He is longing to heal every broken place in you. Please make sure that you walk through your past. Take someone you trust, whether it's a counselor or a small group, and go there. Don't let the past rob you of your future. God is faithful, and He is ready to do healing work in your life!

The majority of your answers are B— It's been a rough road for you, hasn't it? Never quite feeling like you had things figured out, always walking around with that sense that there is something wrong inside. Please take the time to come to God with these things. Whether you do it through a counselor, a recovery group, or in the presence of a trusted friend, God longs to shine a light into those places and free you from the things that bind you. Do it now. Don't wait another day.

The majority of your answers are C— There are probably some closets and pockets of hurt lingering in your heart. You don't yet know how valuable you are in the eyes of Christ. He loves you so much, beyond words, beyond life! He gave everything to know you, and yet that's sometimes hard for you to feel. Don't worry; there is definitely hope. Most of us deal with these feelings— especially if we're honest with ourselves. God wants to take you deeper. He wants to take you to the next level of understanding of who you are in Him. Won't you let Him?

The majority of your answers are D— You were one of the more fortunate ones. Your childhood was a safe place for you, and that has given you a relatively strong foundation. That's a good thing. I would still encourage you, though, to take some time in reflection. Are there any pockets of hurt that have been left unaddressed? Things that might warrant a closer look? How about your past dating relationships? Are there things that might be lingering from those? Blessings to you, dear one. And thank your heavenly Father for your early years. What a wonderful gift they are!

Chapter Four

Friendship

When I first moved to the small town of Columbia, Missouri, I was looking for a safe place. I knew that I needed out of the city I'd been in and that I needed to get away from some of the influences (okay, men) in Indiana. My brother and his family lived in Columbia and he was a pastor. I figured it would be a good idea to get around some other Christians, maybe get my act together.

I lived in their home for five months before finding my own place. I was growing, I was getting a real taste for God, and there was this small sense of hope budding up inside of me. I quit smoking, started working out, and began getting involved in a small group. But I made one tragic mistake. I didn't let any friends into my life. I didn't know how to let anyone in . . . or even that I needed to. I had some girlfriends, but we played together. And we hadn't known each other long enough to go to the deep places.

I had it in my mind that girlfriends were an option; a man was not. Girlfriends were nice, fun to hang out with, but I didn't allow them to be the treasures God fashioned them to be. I didn't know that if I truly invested in them, they could keep me out of a lot of scrapes and hold me true to the values I professed. Without someone to help me see, I was completely blinded when my handsome neighbor came knocking.

With a warm apple pie in hand, he came to my door. Beautiful. He truly was. His chiseled face and body took my breath away. I was unexpectedly and immediately attracted. I even wrote in my journal that very night, "My neighbor came to the door tonight with a hot apple pie. He was handsome and kind—that's all I need!"

It wasn't long before Tim and I were connecting over our balconies—calling out greetings, sitting down over cups of coffee that turned into evening-long conversations. He was hurting from a divorce; I wanted to comfort him. Sure, he didn't believe in God, but he was kind and fun, smart and handsome.

I fell. And I totally deluded myself about the truth. My love for God started taking a back seat. Here were real arms, rather nice ones, and I wanted more.

The truth is, if I had let a girlfriend into the core of me before Tim, if there had been someone who knew how much I was growing and how much I loved God, she could have reminded me of that. If I had an accountability partner, she would have had permission to speak into my life and tell me that this difference was too big. That I would hurt, that he would hurt, and to let him go. My girlfriend would have reminded me of my longing for a mate who loved God as well as me, and she would have exposed the desperate need in me that was causing me to make a different choice.

Without that in my life, I continued into the relationship. I hurt God, I hurt my daughter, I hurt him, and I hurt myself.

It wasn't until much later in the relationship, when we were already heavily invested, that things became clear. The relationship eventually exploded, leaving fragments of us everywhere. The cost was high and we paid it in pain.

One of the most important things I could wish for you, fellow believer, is friendship with God-honoring women. I wish for you to know women who love God and love you enough to make you uncomfortable with your decisions. They will not only be another set of eyes for you, they will also teach you what real intimacy looks like, what love looks like, and what God looks like. Friendship offers us a multitude of benefits, and if we want to proceed into healthy dating relationships, we need them right by our side.

Friendship Teaches Intimacy

Jen grew up with six brothers. She learned early that she had to fend for herself and make her own way in the world. As she grew older, she took control of her circumstances. She decided when and what and whom she allowed into her life, and each relationship was kept distant from the tender things inside of her.

Then she discovered her first real girlfriend. They were roommates. Debbie was all girl. She invaded Jen's carefully protected heart and taught her about being a woman. She gave Jennifer a safe place to be fragile and reminded her that she wasn't (and didn't have to be) one of the boys. Deb reminded Jen that she was a woman, a gentle heart, and that God meant more for her. Debbie taught her through late night conversations, the kind Jennifer could never have known with her rough and tumble brothers. Deb taught her through manicures and coffee breaks, back rubs and pillow fights. Jennifer learned intimacy. She learned that it was okay to let someone into her world. And that if she did let someone in, it wouldn't automatically mean broken toys or hurt feelings.

Without Jennifer's introduction to safe intimacy with Debbie, she would never have been able to allow her future husband into the breakable parts of her soul. God taught her what genuine, authentic, and loving intimacy looked like through Debbie. Once she knew it, she developed other friendships, a support network that involved several godly women. With those in place she was then able to love her husband from a new place of security and comfort.

Authors Dennis McCallum and Gary DeLashmutt, in their book *The Myth of Romance*, say it this way: "This is the best reason for seeking out and developing intimate relationships before marriage, especially in non-romantic friendships. If we are not successfully loving people at the intimate level before marriage, what makes us think we will be able to do so after marriage?"

Jennifer looked at me with a shake of her head. "Elsa, you need a sister." I wasn't sure what she meant until she explained it to me. "A sister has your back. She covers you when you're not at your best and makes up the difference." She showed me that I wasn't letting anyone help me, that I wasn't asking for help, and that I didn't know how to depend on anyone to walk with me in life. She opened my eyes. The truth is, without knowing that we can count on the people around us, without discovering that friends will be there when it hurts, we won't ever learn to lean into the men in our lives. We won't be vulnerable, we won't ask for help, we won't grow in intimacy the way God intended for us to know it, in a way where there is an interdependence of needs expressed and needs met . . . on both sides.

Friendship teaches us how to ask for love, how to receive love, how to give love. Obviously, friendships are not as rosy as all that. But they can be. With the right people who share God's heart, friendship can be one of the greatest treasures of all time. Friendships can offer an environment of safety and joy where we can learn the true meaning of love.

Friendship Offers Accountability

After the break-up with Tim, I really began growing into the faith I had once claimed as everything. I asked after, sought for, and longed to know my God. And He met me. He met me through a variety of sources, but most important to me was the way He met me through my friends.

As I began to grow in being a friend and receiving friendship, I asked for accountability. That had always been a foreign word in the past, something that sounded good but seemed absolutely unrealistic. How did I go about it? What did it look like? Yet I knew with absolute certainty that without accountability I would waver at the first set of piercing blue eyes set in a male body. So I invited people to call me on my weakness. "If I look like I'm getting a little green around the gills . . ." "If I go for someone who isn't what I've said I want . . ." Don't let me, talk to me, remind me, pray with me.

And they do.

If there aren't people in your circle of friends who will tell you the truth, even when it's hard to hear, please do something about it. I've said it in past chapters, and I'll say it again: we were never meant to journey this road alone. Not one of us is immune to making a really dumb move somewhere along the line. The only way to prevent that is to surround ourselves with people who know our weaknesses.

When we're going too fast . . .

Humbly go to mature, safe friends and ask them to tell you when you're getting weird. When they see that crazed look in your eye, and you are preparing to heavily invest in someone quickly, give them permission to say, "Stop!"
—Dr. Henry Cloud and Dr. John Townsend, *Boundaries in Dating*

When we can't see . . .

Because there is so much to know and learn about yourself and another person, you need help in the awareness process. We all have blind spots in regard to ourselves or another person that are invisible to us. We need other people to point out the problem areas that we might otherwise overlook or minimize.
—Dr. Don Raunikar, *Choosing God's Best*

We may have blind spots—things that remain invisible to us about ourselves or the person we love. That's where parents and friends become crucial to us. They know us well— better than anyone else knows us. . . . Without their help, we may march boldly into dangerous territory.
—Dr. Neil Clark Warren, *Finding the Love of Your Life*

Other than your own intimate love relationship with God, nothing will keep you out of relational trouble better than having someone hold you accountable for your words, actions, and intentions.
—Dr. Don Raunikar, *Choosing God's Best*

Wounds from a friend can be trusted. —Proverbs 27:6

Friendship is not only helpful when we need to put on the brakes or run, but friends can also encourage us when it is time to step forward and risk. There are those of us who hide from intimacy and may walk away from a potentially wonderful relationship. An accountability partner can catch us in our excuses and nudge us ahead.

Accountability is key to the foundational health of any budding romance. Don't be afraid of it; rather, embrace it with both arms. The wise counsel of a trusted friend can save us from tremendous amounts of pain or encourage us into a bright relational future.

Friendship Reduces Unhealthy Need

When Tim came knocking, I was vulnerable. Without a lot of friendships in the area, my longing for connection and intimacy was deep. So when his smiling face, listening ears, and warm touch entered my world, it was like a black hole of need was exposed. I wanted to be with him. I wanted to be with him all the time. Instead of progressing at a normal rate, our relationship became serious very quickly. We began spending every free moment of time together, and the fact that we were neighbors did nothing to help the situation.

Tim was meeting almost every need—friendship, companionship, touch, conversation, comfort, protection, warmth. Yet he was never designed to be my everything, nor was I designed to be his. Of course we talked about these things and even sounded good in the expression of our commitments to health. But our daily connection revealed an unhealthy dependence.

Friendships take up the slack where romantic relationships fall short. They keep us from losing our focus, going too deep, or becoming overly dependent. When we don't have some close friendships, we tend to invest everything into the romance. This creates a tremendous risk because when the relationship ends, we will have lost all relational connection. The devastation at that point can seem unbearable.

Maybe you have some close friends. That's a good thing. The second rule to keep in mind, then, is the importance of holding onto those friendships for dear life. Many women may have close friendships but abandon them when a man enters their world. Jenny had three women friends that she connected with regularly. But when Rob came into her life, she wanted to use every available moment to nurture that relationship. She called off their girls' nights, and when she did get together with her friends, she spent all of her time talking about Rob. Her friendships suffered. Eventually, she saw less and less of her friends and more and more of Rob. When the relationship ended, she was startled to realize that there was no one left to help pick up the pieces.

Maintaining our friendships has to be priority in our lives! Dr. Henry Cloud and Dr. John Townsend suggest the same in their book, *Boundaries in Dating*: "Stay involved with your friends and community as an individual, just like you were before you were dating this new person. You are still friends. . . . Don't even attempt to get serious in a dating relationship until you are connected to a good support system and friends who know you. If you are dating from a vacuum, you are in great danger."

We need our friends to help meet our needs and to ensure that our dating life doesn't consume us completely. I was teaching a workshop at a singles conference recently when one woman spoke of it this way: "I know I'm getting in too deep if he's taking up my TV screen." I looked puzzled, but she continued, "I imagine my thought life like a TV screen. If his face is consuming the whole picture, I know that I'm out of balance and I need to redirect my attention to the other priorities in my life."

Is the man in your life filling up your TV screen? Are there some friends that are missing you? Call them . . . today!

I have several good friends in my life right now. They each offer me something different and fill a unique need in my life. I'm holding onto them! When I date, I keep them near. I enjoy my time with them and never sacrifice it in lieu of spending time with a man. There is simply no substitute for what we offer to each other, and I don't ever want to risk the loss of their company. Now should a handsome neighbor come to my door with a hot apple pie . . . and should I be tempted to drink gallons of coffee over hours of conversation, I can remind myself that Donna cooks a mean peach pie, Jennifer makes amazing espresso, and Gretchen makes me laugh like nobody's business. I can think of Carol's wonderful shoulder rubs and Denise's warm smile and good conversation.

And I would accept his warm apple pie with a smile (like I wouldn't take free pie?) and send him off to a life free from a black hole of broken and desperate need.

Building Friendship

It's all well and good to say that we need to cultivate friendship in our lives, but accomplishing that can be an entirely different matter. Where do we start? Who do we include in our lives? How do we make "it" (that warm fuzzy connection) happen?

Perhaps you already have a few friends in your life, but you would like to enrich those relationships. Or maybe, like I experienced, you are in a new town starting from scratch. Wherever you are, one or more of these suggestions may help.

Be wise. It's very important to develop deep friendships with those who share our values. If we are going to ask someone to speak into our life, we want to make sure that what they speak comes from the same source of wisdom we rely on. I love people from every walk of life and really enjoy the diversity in my friendships. Yet there are only a few people whom I will entrust with the deepest parts of me.

We need to make sure that the people we are connecting to on that level will point us to the Father's heart.

Environment. How do we find these jewels? It all depends where we're spending our time. For me, I found some incredible ladies through the women's ministry at church, found a couple hanging out in my neighborhood, and a few here and there throughout the community. Yet most of my closest friendships have developed through the church. These friends are real, authentic, genuine, and fun. They don't profess to be perfect, nor do they put on airs. They simply love God and are pursuing His heart.

I want to be frank with you. Church is a place for broken people who long for God. If you go to a church where everyone has already "arrived," it will be difficult to grow and very hard to find people to connect with on a heart level. Not that church services are necessarily the place to discover these things . . . but small groups are. All churches should have safe places where people have the chance to grow spiritually and deepen relationally. Look for those places and set yourself right in the middle of them. If you want the kind of friendships that are beautiful and worthwhile, put yourself in places where you will encounter other women looking for the same thing.

Getting real. It always feels tremendously risky to expose the things inside of us. I think one of the greatest lies that Satan feeds to us is that we are alone in our fears, sins, and hurts. He doesn't want us talking to one another, for the more isolated we feel, the more likely we are to be distracted from God's truth, hope, and love. What would it feel like to combat the lie? I believe it means taking the time to truly get to know our friends and to not be afraid of sharing the hurts in our lives. For example, imagine that you go to a small group. Across the room is a woman with a bright smile and kind eyes. There seems to be an immediate connection between the two of you. You invite her out for coffee and a friendship begins to flourish. How can you make sure that the friendship has the best chance to grow?

In *Finding the Love of Your Life*, Dr. Neil Clark Warren talks about four principles that can help to build friendship and intimacy between two people.

Interest—People must be assured you really want to hear from them. . . . Studies on intimate sharing indicate that "not really listening" is the most fundamental error people make.

Commitment—The very deepest kind of sharing can take place only when there's no fear of rejection or abandonment. People need to know you are committed to the relationship before they'll open up.

Camaraderie—People who reveal their emotions need to know you genuinely like them.

Participation—Persons who genuinely love each other and seek a deep relationship actively participate in the intimacy process. They sit forward, maintain eye contact, and ask probing questions and guide the discussion with comments. Intimacy happens best when two people listen carefully to each other, convey their support to one another, and totally refrain from judging.

I want to add a fifth dynamic to these principles. *Risk.* Share from the heart. If you are scared to share something, begin by expressing your fear. Let them know you are taking a risk and then plunge in. You could start by saying, "I'm a little nervous about sharing this with you, but I really want to be real in our friendship. This is what is really happening in my life . . ." Think of the times in your life when someone has risked that kind of intimacy with you. Doesn't it build your bond to them? If they have shared their heart with you, doesn't it build your trust in them, your appreciation of the vulnerable place they are coming from? When you open yourself up, rather than scaring people off, you can draw them near.

Having fun. It's great to have long, deep, profound

conversations, but there's nothing like a good solid laugh to bind people together. Especially with women. Get us laughing about the unique attributes of womanhood and there's no stopping us. Go to a good movie, get your nails done, drink hot chocolate on a cold afternoon and discuss your most embarrassing moments, go bowling, take a walk, rollerblade, swing at the park. Take the time to play. We need that as much as children do, and sometimes it's in the midst of a deep belly laugh that you look up and discover that the most interesting thing has happened—you have found a friend.

Bottom Line

Some of these tools will come very naturally to you as you affirm the friendships that are growing in your life. It's the stuff that loving people is made of: a little risk, a little time, some heart listening and laughter. Yet we all need reminders of how important friendship is and how we can work to make it better.

Friendship is so important, especially when we enter into the dating realm. We desperately need good friends who will go the distance with us, who will risk telling us the truth, who will love us enough to stop us in our tracks when we are heading in the wrong direction. That doesn't mean that our friends are always right, but it does mean that their perceptions will always bring our thinking to a deeper level. They may save us from some dire mistakes or push us toward some wonderful gifts. We need them, they need us.

✿

Here are a few questions to see where you are in the realm of friendship; answer them honestly.

✿ **When I have a need in my life (for chicken soup on a day with the flu, for help with groceries):**
A. There is no one I feel like I can call.
B. I'd be scared to call one of my friends; we don't usually ask things of each other.
C. I have two or three people I could comfortably call.
D. I tend to help others but have a hard time asking for help myself.

✿ **When it comes to accountability:**
A. Accountability? I can't think of anyone I could be accountable with.
B. My friendships are more on the surface; we don't ask the hard questions.
C. I meet with someone once a week to keep a check on each other's lives.
D. I've been able to share into the lives of others but have a hard time receiving that.

✿ **If I were to begin dating someone who wasn't good for me:**
A. No one would care.
B. None of my friends would say anything; they'd be too scared to hurt my feelings.
C. My friends would stop me in my tracks!
D. I'm not sure if I would even share that part of my life with my friends.

↬ **When it comes to praying:**

A. There is no one that I know of who is praying for me.

B. In my friendships, we just don't think to ask about prayer requests.

C. There are one or two people who are consistently praying for me.

D. I pray for others but have a hard time asking for prayer.

↬ **When I want to go have some fun:**

A. There are a couple of people I could go out with, but I don't know them very well and don't usually schedule that kind of time.

B. I have friends whom I go out with.

C. I plan fun stuff with my friends—we need it!

D. I don't usually laugh a lot with my friends.

↬ **Most of the people I call friends:**

A. They don't share my values or beliefs.

B. We just hang out; we don't really talk about that stuff.

C. A majority of my friends share my values and beliefs.

D. I tend to adopt the values of the person I'm hanging out with.

↬ **When it comes to church involvement:**

A. I'm happy if I get there once a week.

B. I'm committed to going but I don't really talk to a lot of people.

C. I'm committed to church and to a small group.

D. I'm committed to church and to a small group, but I find myself more in the role of listener.

☙ If I moved out of this town:

A. No one would really notice or miss me.

B. People would miss me, but not for very long.

C. There would be a few people who would feel a genuine loss.

D. I would miss them more than they would miss me.

☙ My friends influence my growth in God:

A. They don't. They are two totally separate things.

B. My friends tend to influence me away from God.

C. The two are intertwined; my growth is significantly influenced by my godly friendships.

D. If my friend is a believer, I tend to grow. When I hang out with my unbelieving friends, I tend to backslide.

Look over your answers and read the appropriate paragraph below.

The majority of your answers are A— Somehow, we have to get you connected! Perhaps you're not really interested in developing some deeper friendships. Sometimes it can feel like that type of friendship is more work than pleasure. Yet there is a rich reward awaiting you if you decide to step forward in this. Or maybe you're new in town and just starting off. Either way, I would encourage you to commit to some type of involvement at your local church, start walking in the mornings with a friend, do something that connects you to other people on a consistent basis. Sometimes the only way that God can reach us is through a close friend. They become "God with skin" in our lives. Please take whatever steps are necessary to build some friendships. Dating at this time may not be wise because you don't have any kind of support network in place.

The majority of your answers are B— It sounds like you have a number of friends, but none of them are really safe places for you to share the deeper things. Maybe you've been afraid to risk being hurt, or perhaps there just haven't been the opportunities that you would like. It might be helpful for you to be more strategic in your friendships. Good conversations and deep relationships rarely happen by accident. Set yourself in some places where people are talking "real." The small group environment is a great place to start. If your church doesn't facilitate small groups, you might want to consider starting your own. Just invite a few people over (whom you respect and look up to) and ask if they would like to meet on a regular basis. You can go through a study together, talk about books, share your lives, whatever works! Once you grow in this area, you will be better able to connect with a man on those levels as well, and you will know if you are dating the right one!

The majority of your answers are C— Wonderful! It seems that you have really had the opportunity to sink into some good friendships. Continue working on those and stay committed to them no matter what your dating status!

The majority of your answers are D— You are a good friend to people, aren't you? It's important to you that you are there for others, that you listen and encourage. Yet you haven't risked being vulnerable yourself. I've been there! Sometimes it feels safer to take care of other people than to receive care yourself. And yet God longs for you to know the joy of being loved and cared for. You are worthy of that time and investment. It may take some practice, but the next time you are feeling down, call someone. Reach out. Ask for help. You need to have some people around you who will affirm who you are, who will make it safe for you to be real so that you can grow. It will be hard to build a solid dating relationship if you don't first do this. If you can't ask your girlfriends for help, how much harder will it be to ask a man?

Chapter Five

His First Love

Dawn met Jake during the coed softball season. He was athletic, fun, and handsome. Every time they met up at the fields, Dawn would feel the butterflies fluttering in her stomach. He made her nervous. Every week she looked forward with greater anticipation to their time together.

Dawn was also growing as a believer. She'd become more involved at her church, and she was enjoying a quiet time every morning. She wasn't certain if Jake believed in God or not. He was divorced—she knew that. He typically had a few beers and occasionally cursed, but that didn't necessarily mean anything. Besides, he was always very kind and respectful toward her.

Jake asked her out. The more she got to know him, the more it seemed they had in common. They both loved the outdoors, dogs, and softball. He was successful in his career and seemed to be both intelligent and down-to-earth. When Dawn finally drew up the courage to ask him about his faith, he dismissed it quickly: "I used to believe when I was a kid," he said. "But I grew out of that as soon as I was old enough to think."

Initially turned off, Dawn soon looked past his response. Maybe if she continued going to church, he would be drawn to God through her. When she talked about her faith, he seemed to be listening . . . okay, maybe not *listening*. But at least he wasn't too critical. So maybe it could work out.

Deeper and deeper Dawn and Jake went into the relationship. Physical boundaries became fluid as Dawn came to the conclusion that God didn't mind if she became intimate with Jake. After all, her feelings were genuine; she loved him. Jake was also falling harder for Dawn and became more possessive and demanding of her time. He didn't like that she was involved at church on Wednesday evenings, and she didn't see what harm would come if she just gave up one night of church. And so it went.

When Dawn and Jake were married on that warm summer day, Dawn had no idea that they would be divorced within three years. The warm breeze whispered nothing of the trouble stirring for their future.

Dating Someone Who Doesn't Believe in Jesus Christ

Don't do it. Please don't do it. Dawn and Jake's story is a familiar one. I did the same thing with Tim, the man I shared about in the last chapter. I didn't understand how important this is. Tim and I never married, but we came very close. Many other women have done the same thing. There are so many reasons that we shouldn't date a nonbeliever, but the most important one is the scriptural instruction not to go there. Dennis McCallum and Gary DeLashmutt explain it well in *The Myth of Romance*: "To seriously date or to consider marrying a non-Christian is outside the will of God. In 2 Corinthians 6:14–15, Paul says, 'Do not be bound together with unbelievers, for . . . what has a believer in common with an unbeliever?' The verb 'bound together' literally means 'unequally yoked.' Paul is recalling the Old Testament command in Deuteronomy 22:10, 'You shall not plow with an ox and a donkey together.' God forbade yoking together beasts of such diverse sizes and strengths because the excessive chafing of the yoke would injure both animals. In the same way, Paul says that a binding relationship between a Christian and a non-Christian will be mutually injurious because they are so essentially different."

I love that thought. This is not about judging someone's worth. I remember feeling intensely about that. I loved Tim. I didn't think it was fair that other people were dictating whether we should be together or not based on my belief and his unbelief. I felt like it was a judgement call on who he was as a man. That offended me. When I finally did make the decision to walk away from that relationship, it wasn't about thinking that I was better than him, or more deserving, or somehow holier-than-thou. I left that relationship because I knew that being unequally yoked was *injuring us both*.

Think about it, friends. Every aspect of life is tied into our spiritual condition. How we raise children, how we handle our time, our finances, our dreams. All of that falls directly under the umbrella of our spiritual values. If those values are vastly different, a relationship can't move in *any* direction without a tremendous amount of pain and frustration.

Just an extra thought for those of you who might be as stubborn as I was about this. I can remember when I was longing for Tim that I looked to find people who would tell me that we were okay. I wanted people to let me know that it would work out. I asked only those who I knew would answer as I wanted them to. It didn't help the situation. The only thing that my selective listening skills gave to me was an even greater depth to the heartbreak after all was said and done.

Don't delude yourself on this one.

Here's one more true story on this topic to remind you not only of the truth, but of God's faithfulness when we are obedient. Julie shares it best in her own words:

"Senior year of high school I was dating the 'perfect' guy in every way for me. Josh was my first love. There was only one significant problem; he was not a Christian. He had been raised by a minister, so he had all of the appropriate values a Christian would have; he just wasn't sure what he believed. I respected his honesty and we stayed together for awhile. Yet it continued to nag at my conscience. After about three months of dating, I realized it was getting too serious. I could see the relationship continuing. I had no way of knowing if his faith would ever develop, so I broke it off."

Julie was sick about her decision for months, losing weight and questioning the wisdom of her choice. It was a painful time. Several years later, she met Jason. He was similar in so many ways to Josh, yet Jason's faith was strong. They were married five years after Josh and Julie split up. God blessed her obedience with a gift in Jason, who was a wonderful, godly man above and beyond her hopes and dreams. "I am so thankful for doing the right thing that time (I haven't always)," Julie said, "even though it felt awful as I did it."

With Jason and Julie, with so many others, God has proved faithful. We can trust that His laws are good. He doesn't want to rob us; He wants us to know His best so that we can experience the best relationships possible. Part of that is making sure we spend time with and marry someone who loves Him.

He Believes... Kind Of

When I met Bill, he said that he believed in God. Nothing in his life reflected that belief, but that seemed to change as we got to know each other. Since I was a baby in my faith, I wasn't looking for more than a man who simply said he believed in Jesus. Bill started coming with me to church, showed an interest in the men's ministry, and began reading his Bible. I was impressed by his interest and saw that as a good sign. What I didn't know to do was to give him the time to develop a faith that was his own. Because his growing interest in God was coupled closely with his growing interest in me, whenever we wavered, he wavered. Several months into our dating relationship, Bill and I broke up. He never came back to church, and I found out later that he went back into his old lifestyle. He had never really encountered God, just me.

If there is a man who interests you, and he is either outside of the faith or just at the beginning of his journey, I encourage you not to date him. If he's interested in God, bring him to church, introduce him to some solid Christian guys, build a friendship. But don't start dating until he is committed in his decision to follow Christ.

More than Words...

Joy also thought she had found the ideal man. He was tall, handsome, ambitious, and spiritual. He seemed to command respect with his strong personality. "I remember when I met Kirk on a blind date to Disneyland," Joy said. "We hit it off right away. He said all the right things, seemed to be a 'godly' man, and was incredibly handsome."

Joy and Kirk began dating. Kirk controlled everything in their relationship. He often spoke of spiritual things but didn't seem to reflect the love of God to those around Him. His spirituality was cloaked in superiority. Initially, Joy was drawn to his commanding nature, but it wasn't long before she began to see the truth. "Something was definitely missing. I began to see that our hearts didn't match. I loved people, he loved himself. I loved learning, he loved himself. It was so weird; what I initially thought was the ideal guy for me was nowhere near what I needed. It was as though God was showing me what it would be like to have my dream man and how miserable and lonely I would be."

Eric was Joy's dearest friend. He was loving, patient, gracious, and kind. "There he was, quietly under my nose," Joy smiled. "He listened to me, hurt with me, and did ministry with me. I loved his heart. It beat just like mine for God and others. When I grew through something, it seemed like it was Eric whom I shared it with and not Kirk. Eric seemed to care about my heart, my dreams, and my spiritual condition more than Kirk. The problem was that Eric was 'just' my friend. He didn't look the part that my husband was to be. He didn't dictate my life like I thought it was supposed to be dictated. He accepted me and loved me for who I was with all my flaws and passions."

A man of godly character will reveal that character through the fruit he produces, not simply through the words that he says. Appearances can be deceiving. It's important to look beyond the words and see what is actually happening in his life as a product of God's presence. It worked for Joy and Eric. They have been married for nearly ten years now. They have four children, and their similar hearts for God and ministry continue to compliment each other and bring light to the world around them.

So How Do You Know?

Begin by stating the obvious. In the beginning of most relationships, it will be our tendency to highlight all that is even remotely good and downplay everything that might appear to be a red flag. Most all of us enter into relationships with a perspective skewed by longings, desire, and hope. Recognize that in yourself. Be discerning in spite of that. We truly need to do our best to keep our feet on the ground and look at our dates with both eyes open.

Look for fruit.

The fruit of the righteous is a tree of life. —Proverbs 11:30

By their fruit you will recognize them. Do people pick grapes from thornbushes, or figs from thistles? Likewise every good tree bears good fruit, but a bad tree bears bad fruit. A good tree cannot bear bad fruit, and a bad tree cannot bear good fruit. . . . Thus, by their fruit you will recognize them. —Matthew 7:16–20

But the fruit of the Spirit is love, joy, peace, patience, kindness, goodness, faithfulness, gentleness and self-control. —Galatians 5:22–23

The good man brings good things out of the good stored up in his heart, and the evil man brings evil things out of the evil stored up in his heart. For out of the overflow of his heart his mouth speaks. —Luke 6:45

He loves God. There is nothing that attracts me more than a man in love with God. I've heard men speak of God, I've heard men pontificate on the virtues of being spiritual, but when I encounter a man truly in love with God, it moves me to the core. There is no denying this one. You can see it. It's in the way he talks, in the way he smiles, in the way he sings and worships. There is vitality in his conversations about God. It's not as though God is a distant being in a far-off universe. A man in love with God speaks about Him as though he knows Him. The matter has become personal, and you can tell. A man in love with God is a find indeed. Don't settle for less.

Such a requirement doesn't mean that he has to be perfect, but if he loves God, he will always be growing, striving, and learning new ways to please Him. If he loves God, he will be able to fulfill the command to love his wife as Christ loved the church and gave Himself up for her (Eph. 5:25) because he will understand God's heart. A man who loves God will not want to disappoint Him. P.B. Wilson, in *Knight in Shining Armor*, says it this way: "First and foremost, is he a man that doesn't want to break God's heart? Notice I didn't say, 'a man that goes to church, studies, and knows the Scriptures.' That's important, of course. However, many of the couples we counsel who are seriously considering divorce attend church faithfully and can quote Scripture. True spirituality requires more than that. When you find a man who is saddened when he disappoints God, you have found a gem. If he doesn't want to hurt God, he won't intentionally hurt you, because that would hurt God."

What a true statement! A man who loves God will be very careful and honorable in how he treats a woman, in how he treats you.

One final thought on his devotion to Christ. For some women, that can seem like a threatening prospect. They want to be first, even before God, in his life. Yet that will only damage your relationship. If his first priority is God, then he will be accountable in his treatment of you. He will desire to honor you even when his feelings don't follow suit. He will be willing to stick with his commitments, and he will walk through the difficult seasons because his love for God will be the sustaining force in his life. If you are at all threatened by the prospect of a man who sets God as his first priority, I encourage you to think through the incredible benefits of his devotion. And take time to make sure God is your first priority. Is there a reason you are threatened by this man's devotion to God? Perhaps God has moved out of place in your own life.

He serves. Wild children surrounded Anna when she met James. It was her first time volunteering in the children's area. He came in with two other children in tow. "Found these guys heading up the hall," he said with a smile. "But I think we have them all now." He'd been serving with the children for more than a year and knew each one by name. While Anna stood still, slightly dazed, James quickly brought order to the chaos. He set some crayons out, laughed with one of the little boys, and proceeded to show Anna the ropes. "John tends to sit in the corner for the first five minutes, but then he'll start to join the fun. Billy and Dalton like to sneak down the hall as soon as their mother walks away. You have to keep an eye on them," he paused and smiled, "but don't worry. They settle in pretty quickly."

Anna didn't worry. In fact, within a couple of Sundays, she knew the ropes as well as James. She also discovered that James was single.

James and Anna began to date. When I asked Anna what she found most attractive about James, she said this: "It meant a lot to me that James had been serving the church for so long. It wasn't as though he was in a high profile position that was getting a lot of recognition, either. He was helping the kids. I also found out he did other things like help clean up the auditorium and stack chairs. When I talked to other leaders around the church, they were very familiar with him. They knew him as a man who was always willing to pitch in a hand, who wanted to help the church in whatever way he could. That was very attractive to me."

This is a big one. A man can say that he loves God and that he's a Christian, but that love needs to be revealed in the way he treats and serves others.

He is wise with money. It may seem odd to place the topic of money into the chapter on your date's spirituality. But this is the exact place for it. Money is discussed throughout Scripture and is closely tied to a man's character. Take a look:

For where your treasure is, there your heart will be also.
—Matthew 6:21

"Bring the whole tithe into the storehouse, that there may be food in my house. Test me in this," says the LORD *Almighty, "and see if I will not throw open the floodgates of heaven and pour out so much blessing that you will not have room enough for it."* —Malachi 3:10

No one can serve two masters. Either he will hate the one and love the other, or he will be devoted to the one and despise the other. You cannot serve both God and Money. —Matthew 6:24

For the love of money is a root of all kinds of evil. Some people, eager for money, have wandered from the faith and pierced themselves with many griefs. —1 Timothy 6:10

I want to be careful here. It is honorable and good for a man to work hard and earn a living (2 Thess. 3:10). I am not suggesting anything different. What we do need to look at, though, is what is first in his life. If he is working solely to get the next house, the next car, the next toy, then he is bound to material things. His heart will not be tender toward God because he has already made the decision about what is most important to him.

One of the ways we can discern a man's financial health is through his faithfulness to tithing. Tithing is non-negotiable in Scripture. Not only that, when we make certain that God's storehouse is full, He is pleased to bless us. What an awesome thing!

You may be wondering how this subject could come up. "Excuse me Joe, are you tithing ten percent?" doesn't necessarily seem like the most graceful way to ask. You can always mention your own tithing practices and even share how God has responded with blessing. What does he say? Does he agree? Or is there a hesitation? Of course, I'm assuming that *you're* tithing. Please make sure you are! Let me encourage you in this. As I write this book, I'm in my third year of freelance writing. I'm also a single parent. I tithe on every penny that comes into my home. My first year as a writer, I made $13,888.00—including child support. Not very much! Yet when I received my financial statement from my church, I had tithed over two thousand three hundred dollars! That means that God brought almost ten thousand dollars into my home through anonymous gifts. I have woken up in the morning to find an envelope of cash on my table. I've received anonymous notes in the mail. Amazing things have happened as God has blessed my tithing practices. If you are not tithing, start now. God promises His faithfulness, and you can literally take that promise to the bank!

The bottom line in this: make sure that the man you are interested in is financially responsible—in his tithing practices, in his diligence as a worker, in his spending habits. If there are red flags in this area, you have probably already noticed them. Please don't put on those colored shades to hide from your concerns. Financial struggles and disagreements are one of the primary frustrations in a marriage. How he handles his money *matters*!

He loves others. Chris was kind, but not to everyone. Sheila only noticed it after several weeks of dating. He was always sweet to her, but when they went out for a meal, he was often rude with the server. He also had a habit of smiling brightly at what she called "the pretty people." When he met someone who was either attractive or wealthy, he had plenty of time for him or her. He would be charming and interested. Yet when he encountered someone who was older, poorer, or overweight, he was quick to end the conversation and find something else to do. Sheila didn't wait long to end the relationship.

A man who loves others, no matter what their story or place in life, is a man who delights God. Throughout Scripture, throughout the parables, the greatest call on our lives is to love God and love others. If the man you are dating has a cold heart, run like the wind!

What If He Has Most of It Right?

We're all growing. Each one of us typically has an area in our lives we are working on. For example, your date could be a struggling workaholic. Hopefully he is aware of his tendency to stay at his job until late in the evening. Perhaps he even understands that he has depended on money and success as a definition of his worth. In fact, many men struggle with this issue because the pressure to have it all is high. The question we need to ask ourselves is whether he is dealing with it. Does he see this as a point of weakness, and is he bringing it to the heart of the Father? Or, if not, is he growing in other areas? It may be that God is working on something else with him. If he is aware of God's hand and is eager to please Him, then you can trust that God will be faithful to continue growing him into the honorable man you long for.

A man who is growing in Christ is not a perfect man. He is an authentic man, real about his weaknesses and pushing forward to work through them. He is a man who does his best to love God sincerely, produce fruit, and honor God with his finances and his actions.

If you are currently dating, I invite you to answer the following questions regarding the spiritual life of your beau. And please remember to remove any tinted glasses as you answer them.

~&~

~&~ The man I am interested in:
A. Does not believe in Jesus Christ.

B. Has shown an interest because of our relationship, but does not have a faith of his own.

C. Has recently become a believer in Jesus Christ.

D. Says he is a believer, but seems stagnant.

E. Is a growing believer who has known God for several years.

~&~ When he talks about God:
A. There is obvious distaste.

B. He seems to reflect back to me what *I* feel.

C. He is just beginning to understand who God is and is trying to grow.

D. He seems to be discussing the news; there is no real emotion.

E. He is animated; he talks as though he knows God personally.

~&~ This man genuinely:
A. Doesn't like God.

B. Likes God as long as I do.

C. Likes God.

D. Says he loves God but doesn't seem to mean it.

E. Loves God!

↬ When I look at how he serves others:
A. He isn't actively involved in any area of service.
B. He participates in the same volunteer activities that I do but doesn't really do things on his own.
C. He has been involved for less than a year.
D. He likes to be involved in the high profile events but doesn't really enjoy serving if he's not recognized.
E. He has been serving for several years and is willing to help others however he can.

↬ When we are out in public:
A. He doesn't have much patience with people.
B. He is kind to those who are kind to him.
C. He treats most people with respect.
D. He seems to treat certain people better than others.
E. He works hard to be kind to whomever he is speaking with.

↬ When it comes to tithing:
A. He does not tithe.
B. He has been tithing, but I think it's just because I do.
C. He doesn't tithe ten percent, but he tithes.
D. He tithes and likes to make sure that others know about it.
E. Tithing is a priority to him; it's non-negotiable.

↬ This man I am interested in:
A. Is obsessed with money.
B. Doesn't have any strong convictions about how he handles his money.
C. Desires to be honorable with his finances and is growing in this.

D. Likes to have the current toys and focuses on material items.

E. Understands the role that money plays and is financially responsible.

↻ This man:

A. Has no desire to spend time with God.

B. Doesn't really spend time with God on his own.

C. Is just starting in his practice of incorporating a quiet time into his day.

D. Talks about his time with God, sometimes coming across sounding superior.

E. Has regular, refreshing times with God.

↻ The man that I am dating:

A. Does not attend church.

B. Began attending church when we started dating.

C. Has been attending church for less than a year.

D. Has been attending church forever; he is legalistic about his attendance.

E. Has been attending church and is committed to its role in his life.

Look over your answers and read the appropriate paragraph below.

The majority of your answers are A— Run! Run like the wind! I know, that sounds harsh, doesn't it? But can I please encourage you to rethink this relationship? I'm assuming that you long to know and please God. Trying to pursue your relationship with God when you are dating a non-Christian will be *very* difficult. It doesn't mean that your feelings for this man aren't real or that it won't be hard to separate yourself from him. Yet it's something I would strongly encourage you to do. Remember the quote from the beginning of this chapter—being unequally yoked will injure you both. Ask God to help you in this process. He is faithful and will give you the strength and the courage to follow through.

The majority of your answers are B— You must have an incredible heart. This man is attracted to God through you. That's a good thing, in that you are obviously revealing the heart of God in a positive light. You should be cautious, though, because he is pursuing Christ based on his relationship with you. You may want to back off from dating him to see if he continues on his own. Is he really interested in God or is he trying to woo you? If this is really the man for you, even if you back off, he will continue his pursuit of righteousness. Then, over time, he may become that godly man you are hoping for!

The majority of your answers are C— The man you are dating is a young believer. You may want to step back from your relationship just a little bit to give him the chance and the room to grow. If you are a young believer yourself, it is possible to grow together; just make sure that you surround yourselves with some extra accountability. Get around a couple that is older and more mature in their belief. Ask them to walk with the two of you, helping you direct your next steps. That will protect you from getting distracted by the relationship in a way that hurts your relationships with God.

The majority of your answers are D— The person you are interested in is stuck. His relationship with God is more than likely based on rules and regulations. His heart may be hardened to the tenderness and compassion of his heavenly Father. This could be a hard road for you. A man who believes in God but rests in legalism will have a hard time loving someone else. It will be difficult for him to admit weakness and therefore be able to grow in real ways. I would raise a high caution flag for this one. And honestly, if I were in your shoes, I would run.

The majority of your answers are E— It sounds like the man you are interested in is an authentic, growing believer in Jesus Christ. He is taking the time to get to know God and understand His heart in all areas. He is open about his weaknesses but continues to bring them into the light of God's law. That's an awesome thing. I would continue to move forward in your relationship as long as you feel God's confirmation.

Chapter Six

His Story

Angie walked into the bathroom and shut the door behind her. She took a deep breath, then another. This was the third time she and Peter had eaten dinner at his family's house. The first time, there had been a small tiff between Peter and his mother. Something about how the chicken was too dry. Angie had attributed it to the stress of having a guest over. The second time, Peter had snapped at his mother about an errand she hadn't had the chance to run for him. He'd been rude and overbearing. Tonight it happened again. Peter's mother was placing glasses of water on the table when one of them spilled over. "Mom!" Peter yelled in anger and disrespect. "You spilled it all over my pants!" Peter stormed out of the room and Angie excused herself in search of the bathroom. She hurt to see the tears springing into his mother's eyes.

Angie could guess where Peter's behavior had come from; he himself had shared about his father's temper and disrespect toward his mother. And yet here he was, doing the same thing. Angie had sensed a temper in Peter, simmering just below the surface. She'd even experienced a spark or two, never expecting that he would get any worse. After all, he was romantic and engaging most of the time. But she knew now that she was deluding herself. She couldn't deny it any longer. If she stayed in the relationship, she would become the focus of his anger and frustration.

Unfortunately, Angie didn't let go. She knew that she should, but every time she went to end the relationship, he turned on the charm. They married. Four years later, they divorced.

Angie suffered because of Peter's story—the one that had shaped and formed his perception of women. The one that left him bitter, angry, and resentful, unable to be a healthy husband.

Just as we discussed in chapter three, our stories matter. His story matters, too. For that reason, it's very important that we take the time to get to know our date's history. What was his family life like? How did he experience childhood? Did he have a good marriage model? Did he grow up in a dysfunctional home? Most importantly, does he understand how his story defines him and what weakness it created?

Peter grew up in an environment where his father constantly berated his mother. While it angered him, Peter had never done any work to expose and heal the wounds of watching that kind of behavior. Because he didn't pursue healing, he ended up repeating the pattern of his father. It's not good enough that our boyfriend expresses anger about the way things transpired in his family or relational history. It's important that he has gone beyond the blame to see what has to be done to grow past it.

Perhaps your boyfriend isn't anything like Peter. It could be that he grew up in the closest thing to June Cleaver's home as he could get. He will still have issues to work through. Robert McGee, in *Search for Significance*, shares how "all of us have a fallen, sinful nature . . . because of that, we all wrestle to some degree with the fears of failure and rejection and with feelings of inadequacy, guilt, and shame. Those from stable, loving families are usually better able to determine what their difficulties are, and be honest about them, than those who are shackled by the defense mechanisms that are often developed in dysfunctional families."

While it may be easier for a man from a healthy family to deal with his past issues, it remains that he must deal with his past. So what are some things to look for to determine whether he has addressed the ways in which he was molded?

Is His Past Shrouded in Mystery?

There are times when I have suffered from what I call the James Dean Syndrome. There was something about that certain heartthrob with the haunted eyes and the shady past. He was the lost one, the one on the edge of the abyss who would probably go over the edge if he didn't encounter the true love of a good woman. Me. There was something appealing about the danger of it all, and if he was distant, handsome, and hurting, I was the girl for him. It's not surprising, really. The bad-boy-gone-good theme has inundated our imaginations from day one. Television shows, movies, books, magazines, all of them with story after story about the broken, mysterious man restored by the charms of just the right woman. Of course in every one of those stories, his past was unknown until the very end. It was something horrible, finally discussed in the climactic scene where he allows the first person ever (me) into the darkness of his soul. After which, naturally, he is healed. A better man. All for the love of one.

Well, it makes a great story but a horrible reality. Perhaps you can relate. Here's the truth: someone who is unwilling to discuss his past is not mysterious; he's unhealthy. He is not a wounded soul in need of your emotional nursing skills. He is in need of much more than you can ever give him.

That doesn't make you a bad person, unkind, cruel, or harsh. It makes you healthy. Think about it. Wounds of a profound nature (the kind your pained mystery man is experiencing) take time to heal. Time, energy, attention, and work. Robert McGee, after discussing those from stable home environments, goes on to say: "Those from abusive, manipulative, or neglectful families have far more to overcome than those from a healthier home environment. . . . Alcoholism, divorce, sexual abuse, physical abuse, workaholism, drug abuse, and other major family disorders leave deep wounds.

"Many people from backgrounds like these have suppressed their intense hurt and anger for so long that they are simply out of touch with the reality in their lives. Therefore, just as a broken arm requires more time, attention, and therapy for healing than does a small abrasion, people suffering from deep emotional, spiritual, and relational injuries need more time, therapy, attention, love, and encouragement than those with minor wounds."

Here's where the hope lies. Robert McGee continues,

"Though the process for recovery may take longer, enjoying health in these areas is still possible if all the elements of healing are applied over its duration" (*Search for Significance*).

A man who has walked through brokenness can know healing, in the same way that you and I can know healing. But it's not your job to *do* the healing. God is the author of wholeness. He brings it to pass when we set our lives before Him (which is another reason you want a man who is after God, because God will be faithful to his completion as well as your own!).

Yet the fact remains that if the man you are dating isn't willing to discuss his past, then he has probably not dealt with it himself. If he's resistant to your inquiries, he has stuff going on that you will suffer from. His willingness to share about his story is a big key to his emotional health. Whether his story is heartbreaking or inspiring, if he is real about it, your chances for success are much greater. So the next time you encounter the mystery man with the furrowed brow and the dark stare, escort him to the door, say a prayer for him, and shut the door firmly behind him. Otherwise, you'll have a whole new series of sad stories in your own repertoire.

Does He Understand How His Past Defines Him?

Janice sat across the table from her date. She could see from Don's posture (hands clenched, shoulders tensed) that he was going to one of the deeper places. "My father expected a lot from me," he began, "and I did everything I could to please him. Of course it never seemed like quite enough." Don smiled briefly. "I got straight A's through school, went on to college, graduated early, and got an excellent job. I did everything right. There were some rough spots, and through those I came to realize that change of any kind tended to throw me. I'll tell you more if you're interested, but what it boils down to is this . . . I fight hard against the impulse to control my surroundings. It's very hard for me to let things happen. I like to know what's coming, and if possible, I like to direct how that affects my life."

Don went on to explain that God had been working with him in this particular area but that it continued to be a struggle. For Janice, his confession was a relief. She knew that if he was addressing it, he had a good chance of actually curbing his need to control everything. She could handle that.

When a man understands how his past defines him, you'll hear confessions like the one above. Hopefully, he will see himself as a work in progress and be able to share those areas where he doesn't have it all together. If he isn't willing to go there, or if he doesn't have anything he sees as a problem, then he isn't being honest or he's in denial. Scripture states that we have all fallen short of the glory of God (Rom. 3:23). There is not one of us who is free from sin. Even Paul, the greatest contributor to the New Testament, stated that he often did things he didn't want to do (Rom. 7:15). No one is exempt; be highly suspicious if someone says otherwise.

Is He Willing to Get Help?

Everyone needs help. At different points in our lives, we all need a set of eyes outside of our own to help us see clearly. Everyone has seasons, years, days where things go wrong and they need a hand. Such a realization indicates strength, not weakness. Yet for many people, getting outside help (such as through counseling, group therapy, or recovery groups) feels too much like weakness, and they refuse to do it. This is a *big one*, ladies. How does your date feel about asking for help? Has he ever pursued counseling for issues from his past? Maybe his past wasn't hard enough to warrant counseling, but how does he feel about the general principle of asking for help? If something were to happen in a future marriage relationship, would he be willing to get counseling?

How Bad Is Too Bad?

Many men have walked through heartbreaking experiences. Fatherless childhoods, abuse, heartache. It's not something to be taken lightly. In *Relationships That Work and Those That Don't*, H. Norman Wright puts it this way: "Many children from dysfunctional families are thrust into adulthood feeling empty and incomplete, afraid and unable to trust because their needs went unmet. And when they don't feel secure in themselves, they look for some type of security outside themselves. They're always trying to fill up the empty space inside. This quest to have needs met leads a person to do one or all of three things: (1) create or adopt compulsive or addictive behavior patterns; (2) make a poor choice of marital partner; (3) place impossible demands upon his or her spouse after marriage."

Not a pretty picture. These are some of the consequences that spring up from dysfunctional childhoods. While we don't want to disqualify someone for things that they had no control over, how they deal with those things now is incredibly important. Are there things in someone's past that should make you run? I don't feel comfortable making any kind of blanket statements. "If he has been divorced twice, run . . ." "If he suffered abuse, run . . ." That doesn't seem fair. Yet if those things have been part of a man's past, how do we know that we won't suffer from the lingering wounds?

Here are some other things you can look for, signs that will help you know whether you can move forward comfortably, or whether you should take a step back. These signs will also be helpful in studying a healthy man. They are universal coping techniques that can either serve as a red flag or a green light and help to ensure that you are *not* settling for less than God's best.

Acceptance versus Bitterness

"I loved her," Nate said. "It broke my heart when it ended, especially since she left so abruptly, without a goodbye. It was as though I had never existed, as if 'we' had never existed. It was a long, hard road to recover from that. And I don't know that I'm fully there yet. I was so angry at first, and I had to bring that anger to God. I knew that if I didn't, the bitterness would rob me of any chance to love again."

Nate knew pain. His wife left in the middle of the day, while he was at work. With no real idea that it was coming, Nate suddenly found himself in divorce court. He had every right to be angry, he had every reason to feel cut to the bone and cheated. Because he had been. But he had choices of where to go with those feelings. He could stay there, stuck in the unfairness of it all, and determine in his mind that love was a worthless pursuit. Or he could fight against bitterness and ask God to keep his heart soft. Nate chose the latter route.

Bitterness is easy to spot. It comes in the form of snide remarks, harsh judgments, and an unwillingness to open up. It also has a way of creeping into other areas of our lives. Someone who is bitter about their childhood can spill anger out onto his children. Someone who is bitter toward a friend can allow gossip to define her conversation. Bitterness robs people of light, and it's not very difficult to see this particular darkness in their eyes. Ephesians 4:31 instructs each of us to "Get rid of all bitterness, rage and anger, brawling and slander, along with every form of malice." If bitterness is running rampant in your Romeo, it won't be long until you will be lumped in with the many who have already disappointed him. See it as a red flag.

If, however, your date refers to different heartaches in his life with an openness that acknowledges hurt but doesn't get stuck there, take hold of his arm and walk another step together.

Responsibility versus Blame

John had an excuse for everything. He was angry in his teens because his father didn't understand him. He was grumpy in his early twenties because he was doing his time in the military. "As soon as I'm out from under these guys, it'll be a lot different." He got out. He soon had a job in a factory, training for management. "As soon as I'm a manager, I won't be so mad all the time. It's just that none of these guys know what they're doing!"

John fell in love. He swept his girlfriend off of her feet with an aggressive pursuit. He was grumpy every so often, but "If you would just say you would marry me, it'd be okay. It's this 'Yes, I love you but no, I'm not ready' that makes it hard for me to see straight."

John got married. He blamed taxes for his financial situation, blamed his boss for his ulcer, blamed his wife for his disorganization. "If only she kept things in order," he would say, "then maybe we wouldn't get behind on the bills."

John didn't stop there. His parents, his lack of money, his wife, his job, his friends, his lack of loyal friends, the moon, the sun, the way the grass needed to be cut every week. Horrible! And all designed specifically to drive him crazy.

Responsibility. No matter what his story, see if your man is taking responsibility for his part of it. Is he acknowledging where he made mistakes? Is he willing to confess that maybe he wasn't that angel of light in his teenage years? Does he understand how he contributed to his own brokenness? This is huge. If your date is spending a lot of time blaming others for his own feelings of pain or frustration, then he will ultimately blame you. It's not even a question; it's inevitability. Perhaps you think that it will be your heart that will be the one he can count on, the one thing that will be right in his life. It won't be. You will let him down, too. Even if you do everything perfectly (and you won't), the blame will land squarely on your doorstep.

I encourage you to make sure that your boyfriend is willing to take responsibility for his own actions. An honorable man will readily acknowledge that he hasn't been perfect, that he made mistakes and hurt people and relationships. We all have.

Coping versus Addictions/Compulsions

I struggle with an addictive personality. I started smoking when I was twelve and didn't stop for far too many years. I am sometimes overly attracted to chocolate, and I can hide easily in a good novel for a period of days. I have various hiding places that God has graciously (and sometimes not so graciously) routed out of my system . . . and I know that without staying in close touch with His heart, I can easily fall into those places again. It is painful to deal with the hurts of life, but I have since learned that it is better to deal with them than to hide. Do I always do it? No. But I try, and I continually depend on God to bring me to the next step of healing.

In addition to dealing with these things myself, I have also dated addicts who are recovering. Before I knew better, I even dated those in the thick of it. Nothing like a pair of addicts spending time together in the midst of their addictions. The priorities run clear. Addiction first, self second, partner third, God . . . last. It's a painful thing. An addict will do whatever it takes to satisfy the yearning for her addiction. Often at the expense of those she cares for.

Is there such a thing as a healthy addict? I believe so. If your date has struggled with addiction in the past, acknowledges that dependence, and has his heart fully in the hand of God, that can even be a good thing. A recovering addict understands how deeply he needs the Father's touch. He is dependent on Him for every healthy step and tends to draw close on a consistent basis. If he is dealing with the hurt in his life and expressing emotion, that's a good thing. Even better if he has a support network of friends who can walk with him when the going gets tough, people who won't let him slip back into old patterns of behavior (more on that in the next chapter). If your date is a practicing addict, I would suggest (strongly) that you separate yourself now. You will not be able to make him better.

A thought to remember with this: addiction is not only about chemical abuse. Your date could be addicted to work, addicted to TV, addicted to you. Keep an eye out for extremes and see what he does when he's experienced a hurt. Does he acknowledge it? Block everyone out and turn on the sports channel? Go grab a six-pack? Even spirituality can be an addiction. If your date experiences a painful circumstance and never deals with the emotion involved, if he calmly states that it's all about God and he's fine no matter what . . . question that. God gave us emotions so that we could deal with the hurt of life. They are meant to be expressed in healthy ways in safe environments. Watch how your date processes through tougher circumstances. If he is refusing to deal with things, don't ignore the red flag. His refusal will spill over into relational conflicts as well. If he is doing his best to handle those emotions, to express and work through them, celebrate. And take another step forward.

A Man with a Vision

Frank was stuck. He was a believer, but that was it. He'd grown up in a Christian home but later encountered some painful experiences. On top of that, he made some poor choices and finally, after years of rebellion, he came back to the heart of God. But that was it. He spent most of his time reflecting on all that had gone wrong. The truth that God had a future and a hope for him was lost in his reflection on all that had happened in his life. He couldn't see forward, he could only see back. And Lena, who loved him, couldn't make him look at it any differently. "I saw all these amazing things in him," Lena said. "But I knew that he had to see them for himself. He was too focused, though, on what had gone wrong. It was like his past was a huge wall in front of him, preventing him from ever having a future."

It's hard for any of us to grasp the grace of God—such incredible grace that He would give us the keys to a bright future no matter what our past looks like. Such truth hides from each of us until we are willing to accept the gift. Unearned, undeserved . . . the gift of hope.

You need a man with hope and a vision for the future. His past may be redeemed, but is he looking toward a future? Does he believe that God has something for him? Proverbs 29:18 says it this way: "Where there is no vision, the people perish" (KJV). A man without vision, without eyes looking forward, can only see what has happened before. And if you love him, it will break your heart.

Pieter, my big brother, knew brokenness. He made poor choices in his youth and spent a number of years seeking all the wrong things. It nearly destroyed him. When he accepted Christ, everything turned around. He could have, very easily, sunk into a place of "what might have been." He could have spent years going over the ways in which he disappointed our parents or the church. Instead, he did the most incredible thing. He accepted

God's gift of a future. Right now, Pieter is pastoring a church of 2,000 people, and his brokenness has become his greatest asset. People can relate to him because when he talks of the saving grace of God, he talks from the heart. But Pieter couldn't do what he's doing if he didn't (1) believe God and (2) dream big. He has a vision.

I think of David in the Bible. He was a broken man, his past littered with betrayal, adultery, and murder. And yet, God called him a man after His own heart. Why? Because David believed God. He believed His goodness, he believed His character, and he believed in the vision God planted in his heart. A man without a dream stays stuck in the past. A man with a dream, not unlike King David, can change the world.

Where is your current beau in the scheme of things? Is he a man with a past? Did he have a healthy childhood? Has he dealt with his "issues"? Here are a few questions that can help define whether your date understands his past in a way that will serve your future together.

⋄ When I ask my date questions about his past (sharing):

A. He says everything was fine, but I don't really believe him.

B. He does the mysterious routine; he doesn't like to talk about it and gets angry when I press it.

C. He talks about his past. It was hard for him, but he expresses that.

D. He had a good past and is willing to share about it (and I believe him).

❧ **If I were to ask my date how his past affected him (awareness):**

A. He would shrug it off. He feels like it's behind him; it doesn't matter now.

B. He would say that it damaged him, but he wouldn't go any further.

C. He would acknowledge that it affected him severely but that he's aware of his weaknesses.

D. He would say that it both strengthened and hurt him, and he knows in what ways it did both.

❧ **If I were to bring up the subject of counseling (getting help):**

A. He would see no need for it.

B. He would get angry and say that his business is his own.

C. He has been to counseling and knows the value of another's opinion.

D. He hasn't been to counseling but would go if the situation called for it.

❧ **When he talks about his family (acceptance):**

A. He talks as though everyone was "nice." There's not much feeling there.

B. He comes off bitter and angry; he doesn't care for his family members.

C. He was hurt by his family but has worked hard on the forgiveness process.

D. He loves his family and easily acknowledges both their positive and negative influences on him.

↪ **When he talks about past romantic relationships (acceptance):**
A. He says that they ended but doesn't express much emotion. "They just weren't right for me."
B. He talks with hardness in his voice. If they hurt him, he has held on to that hurt.
C. He's been hurt by past relationships, but he has worked through to forgiveness.
D. He talks about his past relationships respectfully; there is no bitterness there.

↪ **When he talks about his childhood experiences (responsibility):**
A. He says that his childhood was pretty easygoing; he didn't get in much trouble . . . or at least nothing worth talking about.
B. He blames his parents and his siblings for the pain and frustration he experiences now.
C. He had a rough childhood but admits that he made a lot of poor choices in the process—and takes responsibility for those.
D. He had a solid family but can think of different occasions when he made mistakes.

↪ **When he talks about past romantic relationships (responsibility):**
A. There is no one thing he can pinpoint that didn't work out. They just drifted apart. With a shrug, "That's the way it goes."
B. He blames his ex-girlfriends for the demise of their relationships.

C. He contributed to the breakdown of the relationships and freely admits his role.

D. He can pinpoint the exact reasons that it didn't work out and speaks respectfully of his former girlfriends.

☙ When it comes to addictive or compulsive behaviors (coping):

A. He is an addict and doesn't see it as a problem.

B. He is an addict, and though he may see it as a problem, he justifies it by the circumstances around him.

C. He is a recovering addict who is dependent on the hand of God.

D. He has no addictions that I can see.

☙ When my date encounters a difficult situation (coping):

A. He runs.

B. He gets angry and flies off the handle.

C. His initial response is strained, but he is usually able to take some time to think it through and later deal with the emotion.

D. He is typically self-aware, understands the value of emotions, and expresses them appropriately.

☙ When my date looks toward the future (vision):

A. He doesn't have a vision for his life.

B. He talks of the things he would do, if only . . .

C. He is willing to receive the gift that God has given him of a future; he has hope for what God can do through him.

D. He has a vision for the future.

The majority of your answers are A— Can I be completely blunt with you? Since you can't really answer me, I'm going for it. The man you are dating is in denial. He hasn't looked beyond the surface events of his past, and he doesn't really understand how he has been defined and molded by his experiences. There can be hope for him (as there is for all of us!) in that if he is willing to investigate, to dig, he will grow. As it is, though, you may want to step back from the relationship. If he doesn't understand his weaknesses, he may very well attribute any rough times to your weaknesses—especially if you are further along in the growth process and have already laid them out there. There's a high caution flag waving around this guy.

The majority of your answers are B— I understand why you may want to stand by this man, and that speaks volumes about your heart. But there is really nothing you can do for him. His total frustration with life will most certainly land at your doorstep. Your loving heart will not soften his rough edges, as much as you long to see that happen. Remember the Hollywood version of the bad guy gone good, all for the love of one? It's not true. Keep reminding yourself of that. You are not responsible for making his life better. And please remember that a realization like that does not make you any less the loving, compassionate woman that you desire to be. Okay? Walk away now.

The majority of your answers are C— There is something about a man who understands how dependent he is on God. Someone who has been broken and received God's grace is setting himself up to be a minister of that grace to others. It sounds like your guy is growing. He wants to take responsibility for his actions and pursue health. That is a good thing. The only thing I would remind you of is that past hurt does have consequences. And while your date may be healing, there may still be some hard edges to deal with. You will have to decide within yourself if they are things you can comfortably deal with. If not, it's okay to take a step back. If so, then continue to bring your feelings to God as you walk forward gently.

The majority of your answers are D— It sounds like your beau has a good grasp on things. He was one of the fortunate ones, to grow up without the layers of scars that many of us know. The danger with this man is that he may not be as willing to accept brokenness in others. It might be harder for him to relate to those who have walked through the tougher things of life. On the other hand, he may be very aware of his own blessings, which can open him up to that kind of compassion. Overall, though, I think you can safely move forward, continually bringing your relationship and each other to the heart of the Father.

Chapter Seven

His Friendships

Julie connected with Alan right away. She loved the way he would smile at the sight of her. It was a special smile that reached up and spilled out of his eyes. It warmed her. He seemed like a good man from the inside out—someone Julie could imagine spending a lot of time with. He was known around the church, was active in the community, and had a heart for God. Julie was falling in love.

Julie and Alan began spending more and more time together. On nights when they were apart, Julie wondered what he was doing and wished that he were with her. She knew that Alan had a standing commitment to his small group and also spent another evening with his best friend, John. At first Julie was supportive, but she found it more and more difficult to be away from him. She was becoming dependent, and she began to make little comments about the time that he committed to his friendships. In the quiet moments of reflection that Julie sometimes allowed herself, she could see the darkness of jealousy invading her heart. But she seemed helpless to restrain it.

Alan began to pull away from the tight grip Julie placed on his life. He tried to explain that his friendships were important to him, that they would even make him a better boyfriend . . . but he could tell by the anger in her eyes that she didn't hear him. A month later, he ended the relationship.

Years later, after working through some counseling and growing in her relationship with God, Julie understood why Alan broke things off. "I should have been celebrating his good friends, giving him the freedom of his time," she told me. "Instead, my immaturity got the best of me. I was believing a childish lie that if he was committed to other people in his life, he couldn't possibly love me as much as I needed."

Julie's story is not unusual. It happens from women to men and from men to women. The jealousy that initially comes out as a passion to be together later reveals itself as a deep insecurity that can damage any relationship. What should have been a green light for Julie—that Alan was engaged in loyal and committed friendships—actually became a hindrance.

But are there times when there is reason to question his commitment to his friends? Absolutely. There are what I call "good ol' boy" clubs. These types of friendships take precedence over everything else in your date's life, even God. When your date places his friendships over his other relationships, frequently and without regard for his other commitments, that is a warning sign. So how do we know? What type of friendships should we be looking for in his life? What do those friendships reveal about him? Here are a few signs to look for that will indicate how his friendships will affect your relationship.

Commitment

When to Breathe Easy

Let love and faithfulness never leave you; bind them around your neck, write them on the tablet of your heart. Then you will win favor and a good name in the sight of God and man. —Proverbs 3:3–4

Alan and John got together once a week. They alternated between playing basketball and doing a Bible study on Tuesday nights. Both of them were busy men but maintained that commitment as a non-negotiable. What that should have revealed to Julie was Alan's character. If he was committed to his friendship with John, he would more than likely reveal that same type of commitment to their dating relationship. And since John and Alan had been friends for several years, it spoke well of Alan's ability to commit over the long haul.

Of course, not every male friendship in your date's life has to be so regimented. I don't want you to head for the hills if your date only spends time with his friends once a month, or if, goodness forbid, he doesn't actually plan the time at all but remains spontaneous. What you should look for is the heart behind his friendships. Does he take the time to invest in the relationships? Are they important to him? How does he live out that priority in his life?

When to Be Concerned

There are two scenarios in regard to commitment that would warrant some additional investigation. If your date has no commitment to his friendships, be concerned. If he has latched onto you and left his friends by the wayside, chances are he could easily do the same to you once your relationship has become comfortable. If he says he'll get together with his friends and then blows it off, he is being disrespectful to the relationships that should be prioritized. And undoubtedly, the same lack of commitment will be revealed later on in his time with you.

The second scenario that should cause concern is when your man is overcommitted to his friends. Denise and Bill were dating for several months when she needed Bill's help. She asked if he could take a few hours from work. He said it would be impossible. She was fine with that until the following week, when Bill took off a full day to help one of his friends. That one incident may not have proved anything, but the pattern continued. In many different ways it became obvious to Denise that Bill's friends were a much higher priority than their dating relationship. She was constantly left standing alone when one of his friends called to go do something else. Denise wisely got out of the relationship. "It was one of the last straws. I knew that if I married him, I would be spending many nights home alone while he was out with his friends. I needed more than that."

Healthy Balance

This may seem to be a hard place to define. However, I do believe that God gives us indications of the healthy place to be. Think about it. You may feel some discomfort in the pit of your belly when, for the fourth time, you've been left behind as a better offer comes in from his friends. Or you may wonder why he hasn't seen his best friend for three months. Listen to that place inside. You want a man who is committed to his friends, who places them as a high priority in his life. You also want a man who will give you a place of priority as well. And we can't forget our role in the process. If our date is committed in a healthy way to his friendships, we need to be willing to give him the freedom and the encouragement to spend that time away from us.

Character Check

When to Breathe Easy

A righteous man is cautious in friendship. —Proverbs 12:26

Alexa and Jesse had been dating a few weeks when Alexa met his best friend. Jesse and Doug had known each other for years. Doug was a good man, committed to his family, and an accountability partner to Jesse. They kept each other on track and encouraged each other toward good things. Both of them had personal relationships with Jesus Christ and they encouraged one another to keep that as their top priority. After meeting Doug, Alexa was encouraged about her dating relationship with Jesse. She knew that if it were to develop into something serious, Doug would keep Jesse accountable in his actions. That was a tremendous comfort to Alexa, for she knew that if they progressed toward marriage, Doug would help to build their marriage by stressing Jesse's commitment to her. Alexa liked that.

What kind of men does your date hang out with? Who are his closest friends? Are they honorable? Are they committed to their own marriages? The people that are closest to our date will be the ones to influence him the most. If he is hanging out with a man of character, that man will influence him toward the same behavior.

When to Be Concerned

My son, do not go along with them [sinners], *do not set foot on their paths; for their feet rush into sin, they are swift to shed blood. . . . These men lie in wait for their own blood; they waylay only themselves!* —Proverbs 1:15–16, 18

I suppose I should have known better when I met Bill's best friend, Devon. He was bragging about a recent female conquest while Bill slapped him on the shoulder in congratulations. They laughed together. That really should have been my first clue. But I was young, and I thought that's what all guys did. I would later hear about how Devon had cheated on his girlfriend, how he'd been busted and later dumped. Bill would always talk as though Devon was his hero. "He knows how to get the ladies," Bill would say. "He just walks into a room and everyone wants to be with him. Lucky guy . . ." He mumbled the final words under his breath but I heard them loud and clear.

Later on in our relationship, Bill and I got into an argument. When Bill went to Devon and told him of our disagreement, Devon had only one piece of advice: "Get out man. Get out as fast as you can. She's starting to think she owns you. There are plenty of other fish in the sea. Move on." Of course I heard about Devon's opinion in the midst of a heated disagreement: "Devon thinks I should move on." Yada yada yada. After his full spiel, I encouraged him to follow Devon's advice. And I learned my lesson.

If your date has a best friend with no character, it can cause some significant problems in the relationship. Even if he thinks that he won't be, your date will be influenced by his friend's lifestyle. All of us, including the men in our lives, need someone who will point us in the right direction when we get off track. Without that, or when our closest confidante sends us in the wrong direction, it becomes much harder to be a person of character ourselves.

Healthy Balance

I believe that the best man to connect with is one who has several key friendships. His primary friends will be those who direct him to the heart of the Father. They will hold him accountable and grow him in his own understanding of truth and relationship. When he's mad, they'll let him talk it out. When he wants to leave the relationship, they'll press him for reasons and encourage him to work it out (if that is the right choice).

I want to be careful here. While it is important that a man have close friendships that encourage him toward righteousness, he should also be comfortable relating to people on the hard side of life. Jesus made a specific and purposeful effort to connect to and relate to the broken. He became their friend. So this is the catch. There has to be a healthy balance. Your date's dearest friends should point him to biblical truth and influence him positively, yet he should also be willing to build relationships with people from all walks of life. Because that is what Jesus calls us to do!

I hope I'm being clear. We don't want a guy who is completely surrounded by brokenness, and yet we don't want someone who has totally encased himself in a bubble of religiosity. Is it possible to find such a combination? Yes. I've seen it!

Please don't feel discouraged. When I read back over the last paragraphs, I think how narrow our choices become! Remember this. God is a big God. He knows that you long to make the right choice in your dating relationships. Ask Him for discernment in this matter. Ask Him for the eyes to see the truth about your date's friendships. Then keep your eyes open because He will answer your prayer.

Loyalty and Respect
When to Breathe Easy
A generous man will prosper; he who refreshes others will himself be refreshed. —Proverbs 11:25

When his best friend is struggling with sin, he sees the good in him. In conversation with his friend, he listens to his opinions and respects where he is coming from. There are many different signals that will reveal our date's loyalty and level of respect for his friends. The sentiments come in all different packages. We may see it in the way that he speaks about his friend. He may brag on his friend's accomplishments or laugh as he shares a good memory. There is a sense, in the way that he speaks, that he genuinely loves his friend.

If this is the case, there is a pretty good chance that our date will treat us in the same way. He won't be afraid to celebrate us, to talk about us to others, to be loyal and encouraging. Now there are some men (many men) who don't necessarily gush about their guy friends. But you may see his loyalty in different ways. For example, he is there to help his friend move, or he may take him out to go build something when life gets hard. Whatever the case, his tone is positive and the respect is evident. That is a good thing.

When to Be Concerned
A perverse man stirs up dissension, and a gossip separates close friends. —Proverbs 16:28

If our date is quick to bail on his friend, we should be worried. I can remember one date who had nothing good to say about his friends. One was a cheat, the other complained too much, the last was lazy. He was tired of always having to be there to pick up the pieces. He'd had enough. It wasn't long before I fell into similar categories of frustration for him. And I'm sure that when he was hanging around with his buddies, I was the target of his tinted perceptions.

Several girlfriends of mine have related similar stories. Their dates were quick to dump on their friends, to speak poorly about them, to be disrespectful. It seemed that in each of their stories, it wasn't long before that same attitude was directed toward them.

Be careful if your date is often critical of his friends. Obviously he will need to vent on occasion, but be discerning. If he is constantly complaining about his friends, know that he will soon be complaining to others about you.

Serving

When to Breathe Easy

A friend loves at all times, and a brother is born for adversity. —Proverbs 17:17

Jo loved how Vince served his friends. "When they need him, he does whatever he can to be there," she said. "Whether it's a small task of moving furniture or something big like a crisis in their family, he is there. He can't do it for everybody, but he has two or three friends that he would move heaven and earth for, and they would do the same for him."

Jo and Vince dated for a year before marrying. "I continue to be amazed at the way that Vince serves me. What he did for his friends he also does for me. He takes care of our family and is willing to help me whenever I need it. Well," she said laughing, "most of the time, anyway."

If your date is willing to go the extra mile for his friends, then he will likely do the same for you.

When to Be Concerned

Do not withhold good from those who deserve it, when it is in your power to act. Do not say to your neighbor, "Come back later; I'll give it tomorrow"—when you now have it with you. —Proverbs 3:27–28

If your date doesn't help out when his friends need him, that's a huge red flag. If his friends can't count on him for support in tough times, you will not get his help either.

The Healthy Balance

Some of this goes back to our discussion on commitment

earlier in the chapter. We want our date to be willing to help and serve his friends, but we don't want him to be consumed with it. He could be spending all of his time helping Bob with his deck, Joe with his car, and Dalton with his mulching. Obviously, there needs to be a balance. It's good and healthy for him to serve others. Hopefully, he also knows when it's time to ring the dinner bell and take a break.

Play

When to Breathe Easy

The cheerful heart has a continual feast. —Proverbs 15:15

It's a good thing to date someone who knows how to play. If he can call up his guy friends and go play a game of basketball or golf, or if he can go listen to music or build things with his buddies, that is a good thing. A man who knows how to refresh from his labor will be a well-rounded, generally happy man. If he doesn't know how to play or doesn't have any friends he can call, there will be something missing in his life. And with that something missing, there may come a frustration.

Think of it. We all need periods of refreshment and pleasure. Be very glad if your date has some times of recreation with his friends scheduled into his calendar. That reveals a healthy perspective on life. This is an area where we again, as women, need to let go. Sometimes we get into a relationship and think that our date should be having all his fun with us. Let him play with his friends, ladies. He needs it just as much as we do.

When to Be Concerned

If Jack is all work and no play, or all play and no work, be careful. It's a matter of extremes. If he doesn't take the time to refresh and rejuvenate, then the attitude we discussed earlier will be reflected onto us and others around us. If all he does is refresh and rejuvenate with his buddies, you can easily imagine how quickly we would experience boatloads of frustration as well.

Healthy Balance

Look for a man who works hard but still schedules time to play. If he invests in his friendships to play for the sheer pleasure of their company, then he is likely to do the same with us. If he knows the value of spending playtime together, he will be strategic in making it happen. That will make for some good date nights when the relationship has grown comfortable. A man who knows the importance of play will be sure to integrate that into a relationship. And there is nothing like laughing and growing in a love relationship through the sheer joy of spending time together in fun.

Accountability

When to Breathe Easy

Rebuke a wise man and he will love you. Instruct a wise man and he will be wiser still; teach a righteous man and he will add to his learning. —Proverbs 9:8–9

If your date has invited accountability and truth-telling into his life, celebrate! A man who is willing to allow someone else into his life is a courageous and honorable man. It means that he isn't caught up in pride, that he understands he may have some blind spots, and he is willing to be asked the hard questions. That speaks volumes about his character.

When to Be Concerned

Fools despise wisdom and discipline. —Proverbs 1:7

If your date has a hard time hearing correction from his friends, be worried. If his friends can't let him know that he's getting a little off course, then he's bound to move off course. Every one of us needs accountability and community. There isn't a single one of us who can do life well without a little bit of help.

Healthy Balance

Even if your date is not in an official accountability relationship, make sure that he is willing to hear the truth from his friends. Anyone who doesn't understand his own weaknesses will be a dangerous companion. Anyone who thinks he can beat his weaknesses on his own will fail miserably. We were designed by God to engage in community, to lift each other up, to be a part of His family. We were never meant to figure it out on our own.

The Ideal Man

Always, when I go through lists like the one above, I want to save my readers from going overboard. There is no perfect man with the perfect friendships in place. Well, there may be, but I haven't personally encountered him yet. Your date may have a harder time grasping the concept of play. Or maybe he only has one friend, and that friend is a young believer. Or perhaps he just moved to town and doesn't have any friends. What do we do then? Please remember that all of the thoughts shared in this chapter are guidelines. Always prayerfully consider unique circumstances. Of course, if your date falls into all of the "things to be concerned about" categories, then be concerned! Use good judgment, friends. His friendships do reveal a lot about both his character and his ability to genuinely love and encourage others. Look closely at them and ask for God's heart of discernment.

As in the last chapters, I have a few questions for you. Hopefully, these will help you gauge where your date might be, giving grace where needed and understanding where there might be a problem. Be honest!

The kind of men that my date spends time with:
A. He doesn't spend time with anybody.
B. He is working on some friendships with good men.
C. He has a best friend of solid character and enjoys people in general.
D. He has a lot of Christian friends but doesn't seem to connect at the heart level.
E. The men he hangs out with are of questionable character.

My date:
A. Doesn't really have any friends that he schedules time with.

B. Is interested in spending time with a few good friends.

C. Regularly schedules time to invest in and build his friendships.

D. Spends time with people but doesn't ever seem to engage in any depth of friendship.

E. His buddies are first in his life. He spends a lot of time with them.

❧ When my date talks about his friends:

A. He can be negative about people. He always has a reason for not finding a close friend—and it's usually the other person's fault.

B. He is mostly loyal to the positive things in them.

C. He is extremely loyal and often speaks highly of his good friends.

D. He is kind to his friends when they are there but doesn't have much good (or much of anything) to say after they leave.

E. He defends their behavior, even when it's inappropriate.

❧ The way his friends treat him:

A. What friends?

B. They are kind; they have fun together.

C. They are as committed and loyal as he is—supportive of his goals.

D. No one seems to really know him. They treat him with indifference.

E. They would do anything for him. They are very protective, to the point of being jealous of me.

☙ When my date is angry with his friend:

A. He doesn't have friends to be angry with.

B. He is learning to talk about things but is still growing in that.

C. He immediately goes to speak with his friend about what's bothering him.

D. He lets a few days go by and then acts as though nothing happened.

E. They fight harshly and then eventually work it out.

☙ My date has been committed to his current friendships:

A. What friends?

B. For several months to a year—and he is very interested in committing over the long haul.

C. For years he has remained connected and involved with his friends.

D. His friendships seem to come and go; there is no depth of commitment there.

E. He has known his friends for a long time and the commitment seems almost obsessive.

☙ When his friends need his help, my date:

A. Isn't asked for help.

B. He tries to be there for them.

C. He makes the time to help them, especially the two or three that are closest.

D. He says he'll be there but then usually blows them off.

E. Will do anything for them, to the detriment of everything else in his life.

↪ **When it comes to spending time having fun with his friends:**

A. He's more of a loner and likes to do things on his own.

B. He schedules time to go play once in a while.

C. He makes sure that he and his buddies do fun things together.

D. He's always up for a good time, but his friendships stay at that level.

E. He spends a lot of time out with his friends—excessive amounts of time.

↪ **My date is accountable:**

A. To no one.

B. He has a few friends he would be willing to listen to.

C. He has an accountability partner who speaks into his life regularly.

D. He gets defensive if anyone tries to take him to the heart level.

E. Accountability?

Look over your answers and read the appropriate paragraph below.

If the majority of your answers are A— Your date has trouble connecting with people. Maybe his situation is unique, in that he just moved to town, or there may be some other factor that has kept him from building friendships. The important thing is to do a heart check. Does he realize that he needs friends? He may be an introvert and prefer more time alone. That's okay, too, as long as he understands the value of having one or two friends that he can connect with on a regular basis. Even introverts need accountability and companionship! The thing to watch for is if he is depending on you to meet all of his relational needs. That will become a big burden for you to bear. Also, if he doesn't have someone who will speak truth into his life, it will be difficult for him to grow relationally and spiritually. I would encourage you to be cautious in this scenario.

If the majority of your answers are B— Your date is growing in this area. It sounds like he is interested in building up this part of his life and is engaging in the process. That's a very good sign. I suggest doing your best to encourage this growth—give him the freedom of his time and affirm his friendships. It might also be helpful to be a good model by investing and staying connected to your own friendships.

If the majority of your answers are C— Your date really has this one down. He is committed to his friend-ships and to accountability. He has revealed his ability to commit over the long haul and believes in serving the ones he loves. This is a great thing because you will more than likely reap the benefits of such a committed heart.

If the majority of your answers are D— Be cautious here. It doesn't seem like your date has any real depth to his relationships. He may be mostly about the show, about making it look like he has good friends without ever really risking his heart. Jesus had a lot to say about this kind of man, how he may appear to be clean on the outside but is

---

ultimately dirty and broken on the inside. I would pray and ask God to reveal your date's heart in a way that you will be able to discern. And in the meantime, please take a step back. A man who is about the show in his friendships will be a man about the show in your own relationship.

If the majority of your answers are E— You may have been initially impressed by your date's loyalty to his friends. Perhaps it was even one of the things that attracted you to him. But over time, there have been some red flags. When they call, he is out the door, even if he had a prior commitment to you. There may be some character issues with his friends that have you worried. Pay attention to the concerns you have. It's a good thing that he is so loyal, but he needs to honor his other commitments as well. Be wise, maybe slow down a little bit as you ask God to reveal the truth in this. If you're anything like me, you don't want to spend your married life home alone while he is out with the boys. Think ahead and slow down as you consider these things.

Chapter Eight

Spiritual Oneness

Samantha and Paul were falling in love. They met at a community-wide singles event and had been inseparable since their initial connection. Sammy was a growing Christian and Paul was very spiritual. "I'm not religious," he told her once, "but my spiritual life is strong." Sammy understood his reluctance to be called "religious." There was often an uptight rigidity associated with that term.

Their relationship continued to grow. They spoke often of God together during late night conversations and long walks. Paul really seemed to have a grasp on the beauty and love of God. He made comments here and there that sounded a little off scripturally, but Samantha didn't think much about it. She didn't feel like she knew enough herself to be able to confront some of his inconsistencies. Besides, why rock the boat? It felt good to be in a relationship with someone who at least believed in the existence and beauty of God.

Several months into their relationship, Paul and Samantha attended an Earth Day celebration in their neighborhood. They were walking down the street, hand in hand, when Paul began to share something unsettling.

"Isn't it amazing," he said, "how we are all connected in the grand scheme of things?" She nodded. "See that tree over there?" She looked where he was pointing. "That tree is a part of us. We are a part of the universe and we are all intertwined in the portrait of life." Samantha felt uneasiness spreading through her belly.

"I don't know if that's how God intended it," she said quietly. "I mean, doesn't God say in Genesis that the earth is under our dominion? It is important that we take care of it, but to say that we are a part of it, as in *spiritually*? I'm not sure that's right."

Paul was immediately angry. "The Bible? Come on, Samantha. You can't possibly take that seriously. It's a good book. It has some good advice, but it's not the be-all and end-all that some people make it out to be. No, I'm talking about life energy. The fact that we all share it and . . ." he paused. "Well, it's like this. If you were to cut down that tree, a part of all of us is affected. See?"

Samantha didn't see. With his revelation, their conversations went deeper. Paul didn't believe in Jesus Christ at all, or that humanity even needed Him to be redeemed. He believed instead that people were inherently good and that God was a warm, fuzzy, nebulous presence in the sky. Absolute truths and the dimensions of right and wrong were foreign to him.

Samantha felt foolish for not having seen it sooner. She'd been in such a hurry to know love that she had bypassed some obvious signals that they were not on the same page spiritually. She ended the relationship, leaving as a much wiser woman and a more discerning date.

Spiritual Compatibility

Doctrine. There are a multitude of doctrines throughout religious circles. Someone may deem themselves spiritual and have a completely different view of God than what lies in Scripture. Even denominations within Christianity have unique views on the living out of our faith. It is important to investigate in what ways you and your date are similar and in what ways you are different. Obviously, you won't share everything in common with your beau. Unless both of you come from the same church and an identical background, there are going to be some issues that are incompatible. The wise thing is to know yourself. Know the non-negotiable values within your own spiritual walk. A good gauge of those things is Scriptural truth. While there are many ways to interpret Scripture, the basics are clear. Here are a some of the biblical truths that I firmly believe you must agree on to know true spiritual compatibility:

1. Jesus Christ is the Son of God. He gave His life that we might have the chance to know eternal life. In order to know eternal life, we must accept and believe that He lived, died, and rose again, taking our sins to the cross on our behalf.

2. The Bible is the infallible Word of God.

3. When we accept Christ, we are given the Holy Spirit who, through continual counsel, grows us to become more like Christ.

There are many more important and non-negotiable truths that live throughout Scripture, but those above are a few that are at the foundation of the Christian faith. As in Samantha and Paul's case, spirituality doesn't necessarily mean compatibility. Make sure that both you and your date share the same core beliefs.

Style. James was fully charismatic. Worship time in his church meant raised arms, dancing, and abundant expression. Nancy was very uncomfortable in that environment. She'd grown up in a small Methodist church where she was trained in reverent quiet. The volume of expressions she experienced in the church James attended left Nancy feeling frustrated and unsettled. She simply couldn't concentrate for the distractions.

Yet both James and Nancy were committed followers of Christ. They loved God, they cared about people, and they shared many outside interests as well.

They prayed about it. James suggested that they compromise. In order for both of them to feel comfortable expressing their love for God, they sought out a church that would meet both of their needs. James understood that, while he felt strongly about his verbal expression of love, he didn't necessarily have to do that within his church environment. He felt like he could just as easily express himself fully in the living room of his own home. He also knew that if he needed to, he could attend a different service on occasion. It wasn't a critical issue for him.

Together, James and Nancy found a church that was a good fit for both of them. They were able to resolve their differences.

Worship styles, message styles, dress styles—all of these things run within our personal preferences. Do you know his style and are you willing to support it? Do you understand your own preferences? Know yourself in this. For some, these issues are non-negotiable. If that is the case, then make sure that you are dating someone with similar tastes. Otherwise, be open to experiencing different things and be willing to compromise on the things that *are* negotiable.

Vision. "It is of the utmost importance to know a man's vision. If he feels God has called him to live in the mountains to work with the indigenous people and you're afraid of heights, he is probably not destined to be your husband" (P.B. Wilson, *Knight in Shining Armor*).

What is your vision? What is the vision of the man you are dating? Are those visions compatible? If you imagine yourself ministering in a small church in Iowa while he has visions of being the next US president, there may be some conflict. What calling has God laid on your heart? On his heart? Is it even possible for both of you to fulfill your unique callings together? This is something worth thinking about! Pray together about whether or not your futures are compatible.

Spiritual Growth

"I really thought that we were headed in the same direction," Joey said, "until I figured out that she hasn't drawn any closer to God since the day we met. She doesn't do anything to connect or build her relationship with God. Meanwhile, I've been pushing forward steadily and now feel like we are in two completely different places."

Different growth curves within a relationship are typical. Obviously, both people won't maintain the same spiritual development over the same length of time. The thing to be watchful for is the elements of growth. Is your date actively engaged in practices that will promote growth?

Are you? This would include things like a quiet time, devotion to Scripture, prayer, small group involvement, and church attendance. If these elements aren't a part of your date's current lifestyle, you might want to take a closer look at whether you will be able to grow together toward spiritual maturity.

Spiritual Leadership

This is a subject that's been cause for multiple conversations throughout our culture. The role of the husband as spiritual leader and the art of submission are two concepts that have been dragged through the enlightened mud of our communities. Yet Scripture leaves no room for argument.

Submit to one another out of reverence for Christ. Wives, submit to your husbands as to the Lord. For the husband is the head of the wife as Christ is the head of the church, his body, of which he is the Savior. Now as the church submits to Christ, so also wives should submit to their husbands in everything. Husbands, love your wives, just as Christ loved the church and gave himself up for her.
—Ephesians 5:21–25

So you're thinking, *Well, I'm just dating . . . I don't need to worry about this yet!* But you do. We do. This concept is an important one to understand and embrace. If your shackles rise at the very thought of submission, read on. Here are some additional explanations that may help you understand the importance of the concept.

His leadership. "I'm not submitting to anyone!" Julie said to me fervently. "That stuff comes from the dark ages.

I'm not letting any man tell me what to do or dictate how I should live my life. Absolutely not!" I looked at her with understanding. Because of the many ways *submission* has become like a dirty word, many of us are very resistant to the idea. In Julie's case, she had some historical baggage to add to her concern. None of the men in her life had given her reason to trust the thought of submission. She'd grown up with an overbearing father, married an abusive man, and was currently divorced. The thought of giving over any semblance of control in her life brought up feelings of fear and anguish. She was certain submission meant only one thing: pain.

If we are at all like Julie, with such heartache in our past, healing needs to take place before we can even begin to understand and embrace submission. Of vital importance as well is the type of man we set in that place. Obviously, he needs to be a man of integrity and character. I would encourage you to take a very close look at the spiritual decisions your date is making in his single life. Is he a good leader of his own affairs? Is he someone whom you would entrust with the spiritual health of your relationship? Is he encouraging physical purity and obeying God's laws in your relationship before marriage?

Not that it's all up to him, but is he the type of Christian that you would be willing to partner with over the long haul? If, for example, he is compromising on core beliefs that you hold strong and secure, there may be a problem. Ultimately, in marriage, he may ask you to compromise on those same beliefs. My guess is that you already know if this is an area of concern for you. Don't brush it to the side. Remain aware and discerning about how his spiritual leadership will develop in your marriage.

Our submission. If the word *submission* ties you up in knots and brings to mind the image of doormats and timidity, listen to P.B. Wilson, author of *Knight in Shining Armor*:

How does submission work? Let me use a broken traffic signal as an example. Before you drive your car to a destination, you probably don't pray: "Lord, whatever you do, please don't let there be a broken traffic signal at a busy intersection on the way to where I am going!" Why don't we pray that prayer? Because we've learned through driver's education or the driver's handbook that when we come to an intersection and the traffic signal is broken, the first thing we do is stop. We allow the cars on our right to proceed first. Then the cars on their right go, and continue this way until the traffic signal is repaired. Now, what if an order had not been established when we learned to drive? There would be utter chaos in the intersection, and people would be arguing and bumping into each other, trying to prove they have the right of way.

Have you ever wondered why we need the principle of submission? One possible explanation is that God knew He had created freethinking individuals and by nature every person does what is right in his own eyes. He also knew that if any two people spent any amount of time together, sooner or later the communications would collapse—the "signal" would be broken. If an order had not been established there would be utter confusion in the relationship.

P.B. Wilson also shares how the art of submission doesn't begin at the altar. We are all required to submit to certain authorities and laws throughout our lifetime. As

Christians, we submit to each other. If that's been an issue for you in other areas, then this might be a good time to take a look at where you stand with submission in marriage. There is a reason that God sets an order into place. Unless we are willing to follow it, we will experience incredible frustration in our marital relationships.

The pitfalls of leadership and submission. I had a boyfriend who loved the idea of submission. He wasn't a strong believer, and his idea of submission meant that he would say something and I would do it. He had visions of getting whatever he wanted, whenever he wanted. His view of submission was all about power and had nothing to do with love. Be aware of the potential for this type of attitude. A reminder: *A godly man will offer leadership out of his sense of responsibility to God and his desire to protect and honor you.* Watch for his motives.

Remember also to consider your own view of submission. If this is an extremely sensitive issue for you, you may want to do some additional research and go to God with your concerns. Don't get any more serious in your relationship, though, until you have a better grasp on it. This is one of those issues that you don't want to be trying to figure out *after* you are married.

One final thought. You are *not* required to submit to your boyfriend. For example, if he is pushing certain ideas, thoughts, or practices on you and quoting your requirement to submit . . . run! That's not scriptural and it certainly isn't honorable.

Spiritual Intimacy

I was sitting with a friend over a cup of coffee when she

shared her own experience with spiritual intimacy. "My boyfriend and I would pray together intensely," she said. "The depth and richness of that time was incredible. He was a strong believer and I was growing." She paused. "But I discovered something. After a particularly intimate prayer time, I found in myself the desire to take that same spiritual intimacy to a physical level. I wanted to be with him, in his arms, together. The passion that was stirred up in our prayer time was unequal to what I had experienced when I was a non-believer dating another non-believer."

Prayer is vital to a relationship. It's good and pure to spend time in prayer with the one whom you are growing to love. But be cautious! There is an intimacy that is fostered in that environment that can easily lead to other forms of expression. A way to protect yourself in this process is to make sure that you are not praying together in places that leave you open to physical temptation. In my opinion, it would be even wiser to leave intense prayer to times spent with a same sex accountability partner or small group. Pray together, yes. But spending a lot of time in passionate conversation with God in an intimate environment will set you up to continue that intimacy in other ways.

Spiritual Integrity (Through Physical Purity)

One of the easiest (and most common) ways to stumble on our spiritual walk is by allowing our dating relationship to become sexual before marriage. We may begin the dating process with the best of intentions only to let the temptation get the best of us.

It happened to Annette. She had committed to staying pure. She had made mistakes in the past, but within the context of her renewed commitment to God she wanted to do things differently. She met Todd, a fellow Christian, through the church. She felt good about their connection, especially since he shared the same value of purity. For several months they dated, and both were pleased with their restraint. Yet, as their feelings grew, so did their physical desire.

Annette began to wonder where exactly in Scripture premarital sex was forbidden. She found herself rationalizing her desire with different justifications. *But I've already been married. I've already traveled this road.* Or *I'm twenty-eight years old! I can understand why God set those laws in place for a teenager or a young adult, but I'm mature enough to handle this.* Or *What could possibly be wrong in expressing love? It's not like I'm doing something to hurt anyone. This is a good thing!*

Todd was doing the same thing in his own mind. It was a Friday night when it happened. They were watching a movie, cuddling in front of the TV. Their kisses turned to caresses; the caresses continued until they could no more stop their desire than stop the sun from rising.

Once they entered into a sexual relationship, it was very difficult to put on the brakes. So they didn't. Instead, they found themselves withdrawing from church activities and small group meetings. Annette seemed to have a harder time fitting in her quiet times in the morning. Every so often, when she was still, she would admit to herself that she was avoiding God. But the truth was, she didn't really know how to go backwards and wasn't even sure that she wanted to.

It was only a few months later that the relationship ended. Both Todd and Annette now wish that they had made a different choice. "I knew in my heart that God had a reason for purity," Annette said, "but when push came to shove, I gave in. And it hurt us both, emotionally *and* spiritually."

The longing. Oh, how the longing can stir in us. If you are dating right now, you know what I'm talking about. You have looked deep into his eyes and felt the stirring in your belly. Perhaps you lingered over a kiss or shivered at the feel of his hand on the small of your back. It feels good to be touched. It feels good to touch. Intimacy can be created in the simplest moment. A hand held, a warm hug. A connection begins to build. Shared smiles and meaningful looks are exchanged. You are drawing closer and it's an amazing feeling.

Now what? This is the point where most couples make a critical decision. They either continue in their initial commitment to remain pure (if they have made that commitment) and stand firm in their physical boundaries . . . or they allow the feelings to escalate, letting each kiss last a little longer and each caress grow more passionate in its intensity. Which, of course, feels very good at the time, but often leads to growing sexual desires.

So how do we guard our premarital relationships from sexual sin? Why should we stay pure? As a single woman too, let me just remind you that we are in this together. I firmly believe that the *only* way we can maintain purity is with God's help. We need to ask Him for help in understanding why He calls us to wait until marriage for sexual intimacy, and we need to believe that there are benefits to following that path. Otherwise, we will talk ourselves *into* situations or blind ourselves *out of* our values when we encounter the intimate touch of one we are growing to love.

Why purity? Greg Speck, the author of *Sex: It's Worth Waiting For*, cites several different scriptural mandates regarding premarital sex. He does a wonderful job of explaining each one in his book. I will share some of his thoughts as well as add a few of my own.

For this reason a man will leave his father and mother to be united to his wife, and they will become one flesh (Gen. 2:24). God has a specific order in mind for our relationships. First we leave our father and mother, then we are united, *then* we become one flesh. One, two, three. When we disregard the order, we end up outside of His will. And we all know how difficult life can be when we do that!

May your fountain be blessed, and may you rejoice in the wife of your youth. A loving doe, a graceful deer—may her breasts satisfy you always, may you ever be captivated by her love (Prov. 5:18–19). Sex within the marriage relationship has the potential to be a beautiful experience. This particular verse rejoices in the goodness of sexual relationship. Notice that it doesn't say, "May your fountain be blessed, may you rejoice in the one you love . . ." It speaks of the joy in sexual expression within the context of marriage.

Now to the unmarried and the widows I say: It is good for them to stay unmarried, as I am. But if they cannot control themselves, they should marry, for it is better to marry than to burn with passion (1 Cor. 7:8–9). Paul's instruction regarding passion and the fulfillment of its yearning leaves no question as to where that passion should be satisfied. He doesn't say, "Okay, if you're burning with passion and you really love each other, then you can go ahead and fulfill the longing." Paul assumes that the reader is already convinced, that his audience understands that premarital sex isn't even an option.

Benefits of Purity

Throughout Scripture, God gives us a strong foundation for the value of maintaining sexual purity. But there's more. Not only can we experience the sheer delight of walking within God's will; there are additional blessings to be found in purity.

The way we feel. If you are anything like the thousands of Americans who have adopted a diet or exercise regimen, you will understand this analogy. Can you think of times when you woke up before you wanted to, when you struggled out of bed and went for that long walk? Remember the times when you passed up that gargantuan bowl of ice cream at midnight? It was a painful thing to do at the time, and it required most of your strength and willpower. But afterwards, when the temptation passed, there came this sense of accomplishment, a joy in doing the right thing despite the hardship.

Maintaining purity offers that same sense of joy. Deep inside, you know that you have made the best choice. You can walk with your head a little higher, your shoulders set in place, knowing that you have chosen obedience to your heavenly Father and the best course of action for your relationship. It binds you to your dating partner because you have esteemed self-control over self-gratification. You have come to understand that the short-term satisfaction that comes from physical fulfillment is far outweighed by the long-term joy that spills out from obedience. And that, my friends, feels good.

Knowing why he's there. If you are not sexually involved, you don't have to wonder if your date is spending time with you to merely fill a physical need. If after an evening of conversation both of you desire to spend more time in conversation, then it's a good bet to say that you like each other as individuals. When a relationship has become sexual, it's much more difficult to know if he is spending time with you because of you or because he enjoys the feel of your touch.

The development of discipline. The development of personal discipline is key to growing in our relationships with God and one another. And there is nothing like strengthening the discipline muscle through the practice of physical restraint. When you can set aside something that feels so good, delaying gratification, you set yourselves up well in other areas of your life.

Clear vision. Let's be completely honest: Your date may be a wonderful sexual partner and a lousy human being. When you allow the physical side of your relationship to develop prematurely, you don't see well. We can all tend to neglect the warning signs and hide in the comfort of touch. What happens, though, is that you end up investing your heart as you invest your body . . . and when your vision does clear (and it will), you are left with someone who can't love you in the deep ways you long for.

Opportunity to reflect Christ. You have the opportunity to reflect God to other couples as you promote and live out purity. Think of it! There are very few couples who practice that kind of restraint. What a witness you can be to believers and non-believers alike! Basically, you are telling the world that love is more than sex, that God's laws can be followed today, and that it's possible to have a fun, fulfilling relationship without being sexually active. Many would say that such a thing is impossible. Reveal how God's truth works practically in your life and prove them wrong!

How to Stay Pure

It's great to want purity. It's wonderful to long for spiritual integrity in our relationships. But we need more than the desire. We need some tools to take us there. Here are a few that might be helpful:

Both must be committed. As much as we would like to be, we are not super-human. There will be moments when one of the two may be weak. Both people need to be committed to purity. If you are in a relationship now where you are the only one holding on to the boundaries, or if he is the one who believes it while you are uncertain, take a step back. Both of you need to be committed to this value for it to work.

Accountability. Do you have a friend who might be willing to call you the morning after a date? When you know you are accountable to someone, it makes it easier to draw the line.

Action and truth. "Dear children, let us not love with words or tongue but with actions and in truth" (1 John 3:18). We can be all about words. We can talk the talk and, when the moment comes, live something completely different. Sexual purity is the perfect opportunity to live out your love (for God and for your beau) in action and in truth. What does it look like? All that you do within your dating relationship should be done with purity in mind. Think about the things you wear, how you talk, the environment you hang out in. After all, if you're spending all of your date time on the couch watching movies, things are bound to happen. It's good to get out and about. Be aware of your thoughts, too. As a writer I really have to watch this. My imagination serves me well in lots of other places, but I have to be careful when I start imagining what it would be like if . . . .

Common Mistakes

Finally, here are a few common slip-ups that many women have encountered. See if they sound familiar:

"We'll go this far . . . and that's it!" "Well, as long as we don't have intercourse, we're okay." A couple will get closer and closer to that line, doing everything possible except the actual act of sexual intercourse.

Think of this: "Remember that petting is subject to the moral law of diminishing returns. That means the more you do something the less exciting it is. So in order to keep petting exciting, and to gain satisfaction, the amount and intensity of the petting must continue to increase" (Greg Speck, *Sex, It's Worth Waiting For*).

It is nearly impossible to continue touching each other sexually indefinitely. People will either keep going or become more and more frustrated. Why put your relationship through that kind of trauma? It simply isn't worth the momentary pleasure. If you are already in this stage, take a step in a different direction. Be firm. If you truly want this relationship to succeed, give it a real chance to do so.

Then, if this is the one, and you decide to marry, you will have the freedom, the blessing, and the extreme pleasure of touching all you want!

Desire to be irresistible. "Who wants to be resistible?" Jan said to me, half-laughing. "He resists me so well!" Jan was dating a man who was doing his best to honor and respect her. At the same time that his restraint pleased her, she also found herself frustrated. She wanted him to want her. She wanted to be irresistible in his eyes. We all want to be attractive and desirable! But if your man is successfully resisting your beauty, be happy about that. It doesn't mean that you are unattractive or undesirable. In fact, if you are feeling some of those things, I would encourage you to go to your heavenly Father so that He can remind you where your true value lies. It doesn't lie in your womanly wiles, it lies in the fact that you were hand-crafted and lovingly designed by your Creator.

"But we're different!" Every couple feels like they are unique. They believe that their love and commitment is above and beyond that of every other couple in the universe. They are going to make it, and if they have sex . . . well, it's because their love is unusually strong and beautiful. Yes, your love may be particularly strong, maybe even stronger than most, but God set these standards in place for everyone. They've been set in place to protect our hearts and relationships. They are designed because in our humanity we are achingly similar. We long to know and be known. We long to love and be loved.

Often that need is translated into a physical relationship. We sacrifice what is good and pure to know a momentary connection. It's not unusual; many of us share this weakness. I just encourage you to set aside any notion that your relationship is somehow different from all the rest. Know that your Father loves you deeply and passionately. He has more for you than you can even begin to imagine, and temporarily satisfying a need for intimacy will sacrifice His blessing. Don't let that happen! Enjoy your relationship; savor the sweet moments of conversation and companionship. Have fun together, listen to each other, and build good memories. And when it comes to sexual expression, hold off for just a little while longer.

Remember, the spiritual integrity of your relationship that comes through physical purity is so important. Fight for it; give it your best so that God can pour back *His* best into your relationship.

So let's find out. Are you and your date compatible spiritually? Here we go on another round of questions . . .

⤳ When it comes to Jesus Christ:
A. Only one of us believes in the deity of Jesus Christ and that His death and resurrection are fundamental to faith.
B. One of us is strong in the conviction that Jesus Christ is Lord; the other is just beginning to embrace it.
C. Both believe, without question, in the deity of Jesus Christ.

⤳ When it comes to the Bible:
A. Only one of us believes that the Bible is the Word of God; the other thinks of it as literature alone.
B. One of us believes firmly that the Bible is the Word of God; the other is open to the thought but not convinced.

C. Both of us believe strongly that the Bible is the infallible Word of God.

↝ **When it comes to the Holy Spirit:**
A. Only one of us believes that the Holy Spirit is a living and active presence in our lives, transforming us into the image of Christ.
B. One of us believes firmly in the Holy Spirit; the other is a little spooked by the whole idea.
C. Both of us agree that the Holy Spirit is a vital and necessary presence in the life of all believers.

↝ **When it comes to worship:**
A. We have completely different styles of worship and one or both of us is unwilling to give up our particular form of expression *or* one worships regularly and the other does not.
B. We have different styles of worship but are both open to exploring something different.
C. We share similar styles of worship.

↝ **When it comes to our church:**
A. We attend two completely different churches. Neither one of us is willing to give up our current community of believers *or* one attends a church regularly while the other does not.
B. We attend two different churches but are willing to make a change.
C. We are part of the same church or a similar church environment.

ᴥ When it comes to a vision for the future:

A. My date and I have incompatible visions; one could not be fulfilled in tandem with the other *or* only one of us has a vision.

B. Our visions are mostly compatible; there are some differences, but they are workable.

C. Our visions compliment each other well.

ᴥ When it comes to quiet times:

A. Only one of us believes in the value of time spent alone with God.

B. We differ on the way we have our quiet times, but, for the most part, we understand the value.

C. Both of us share a similar passion and style in our quiet times.

ᴥ When it comes to attending church:

A. Only one of us believes in regular church attendance.

B. One of us is passionate about church attendance; the other doesn't see it as a top priority . . . though we both attend on most Sundays.

C. Both of us believe strongly in the value of regular church attendance and are committed to that in our daily walks.

ᴥ The man I am dating:

A. Is not someone I could trust to be the spiritual leader.

B. Is growing in his capacity to be a spiritual leader.

C. Is someone I feel very comfortable trusting as a spiritual leader.

♪ **When I think of submission:**

A. I get creepy-crawlies all up and down my spine.

B. I'm hesitant, but I'm open to exploring God's original intentions when He called us to it.

C. I understand the value of submission and feel comfortable embracing the concept as God designed it.

♪ **My boyfriend and I:**

A. Have had sex.

B. Have been involved in some strong physical activities but have not slept together.

C. Have kept strict physical boundaries.

♪ **We believe God calls us to:**

A. Love each other, even if that means sexual contact.

B. Purity . . . but my boyfriend is not convinced.

C. Wait until marriage before having sex.

Look over your answers and read the appropriate paragraph below.

If the majority of your answers are A— You probably already know what I'm going to say on this one. It's just not a good idea. The two of you are on completely different ends of the spectrum. I would suggest going to the next chapter, where it talks about how to end a relationship. I know, harsh. But it's true. The spiritual side to a relationship is a key ingredient to the joy potential. I'm afraid that you are going to end up experiencing a lot of frustration and sadness. As a fellow single woman who understands how hard this might be for you, I still encourage you to get out of this relationship. Soon.

If the majority of your answers are B— It sounds like there may be some areas of concern for you. That's okay, because there is also hope. A good idea at this point would be to get under the covering of an older, spiritually mature couple. Mentoring can be of tremendous help in unifying a couple with these workable differences. The only caution I would extend is to be watchful. If, over time, the differences between your spiritual walks remain significant, you may want to take a step back. If you begin to grow together in ways that draw you to a similar place spiritually, then you can safely continue in the relationship.

If the majority of your answers are C— It sounds like you two are on the same page! That's a wonderful thing. At this point I would just suggest that you continue to walk forward, being wise and discerning about your compatibility in other areas. Do you genuinely like your time together? Do you enjoy the same things? Sometimes we can choose someone who is very similar spiritually only to discover that we really don't share anything else in common. That would be my only caution to you. Otherwise, I would encourage you to continue moving forward in your relationship and celebrate the unique compatibility that you share!

Chapter Nine

How to Walk Away

Janet knew it wasn't right. Almost from the beginning, she had the sense that the relationship wasn't going to work. It was the feeling in her belly, the anxiety that lingered after she spent time with him, and the irritability that spilled out into other areas of her life. Yet she was so lonely. And he was someone. She knew that sounded harsh, but deep down it was the truth. Even though there were things that really concerned her, each day seemed to flow into the next and she felt helpless to end it. There was something in her that yearned for his company, and she clung to the hope that maybe it could grow into something good.

It was late one evening, after a particularly unfulfilling date, that Janet told herself the truth. *I want him to be something that he isn't,* she confessed to herself. *I keep hoping that he will change into the man that I have always wanted. It's not going to happen and that just breaks my heart.* Janet was tired of looking, tired of being alone, tired of dealing with life on her own. She was willing to settle for someone who would ultimately cause her more harm than good because it seemed better than the emptiness that came from being alone. It was almost as though relating with someone on an intimate level, even if that relating was inappropriate or painful, was better than not relating at all. *At least,* she thought to herself, *when I am with him there are moments when I laugh, times when I feel warm and safe in his arms. And I see, just for a second, what true love might look like.* And for those moments Janet was willing to sacrifice. A lot.

The tears spilled onto Janet's cheeks. She was going to have to end it. She knew that. She dreaded the coming evenings of quiet and the loneliness that would settle in. She wondered if maybe she was expecting too much. After all, nobody was perfect. Plus, with her past, how could she really expect anything more? Perhaps she just needed to give the relationship a little more time. Perhaps it would get better. Besides, he really was a decent guy.

The Truth

Have you ever been in Janet's shoes? I have. It's such a painful place to be. I've known, deep inside, that the relationship wasn't going to last. Yet I stayed. I stayed because I didn't know how to get out and didn't know if I wanted to. Something seemed better than nothing. Even though, at the core of the matter, I was more miserable in the relationship than I had ever been on my own. I held on. I held on until it got to the point where it ended, as I knew it would. Because it died a slow, lingering, broken death, it was much more painful than if I had acknowledged the truth at the beginning. I believe, with all my heart, that most of the time, we know. You know. I know.

The relationship you are in right now, you have a good sense of whether it's right. If the relationship isn't right, this chapter will give you the tools to acknowledge the truth and then take the steps to walk away. If the relationship is right, the final chapter will give you some ways to dig in and grow deeper. May God direct your steps either way!

Is This Relationship Going to Work?

Maybe you've gone through this book and discovered a number of red flags along the way. Yet you are still hoping and believing that the relationship you are in will know success. Before you go any further, walk through the following steps. Ask God to reveal His heart to you.

Be honest with yourself. Anna always made time for herself. As a single woman, she often took the time to reflect on her choices and discern whether they fell in line with her beliefs. Then she began to date Rick. He pursued her fervently. He swept her off of her feet with romantic dinners and words that lingered long after he spoke them. Anna found herself more and more enamored with the man Rick presented himself to be. As the relationship deepened, Anna noticed that she didn't spend as much time evaluating her life. She supposed that was natural. She was just busier than she had once been.

Anna and Rick continued to date. Anna began to notice some patterns in Rick's behavior that made her uncomfortable. He seemed to do everything to excess. He had pursued her with passion, but that same zeal revealed itself in his love for a good time, for drinking, for money. Anna sensed the discomfort inside her heart but didn't want to evaluate it. She started avoiding time alone and conveniently found other things to do. When the questions seemed to surface, she told herself that she was worrying too much, that everything was okay, really. When her close Christian friends asked her about the relationship, she was also less than honest. She told them of all his wonderful traits and simply left out the ones that worried her. She painted a picture for herself and anyone that cared to ask, a picture that was defined more by her own longing than by reality.

When Anna was finally honest with herself, the relationship was a year old and her heart was intertwined with his. The break up left her with many regrets. She wished that she had been honest with herself right from the start. It would have saved her much of the sadness that now seemed to define her days.

Telling yourself the half-truth . . . and being too busy to think. What are you telling yourself about the relationship you are in? Do you sense that you are looking through rose-colored glasses? Are you conveniently ignoring any glaring character flaws? I imagine that as you read this, you'll know if it describes you. Be honest. Are you avoiding the truth? This is big, my friends. We all have to deal with the truth eventually. Would you rather be honest with yourself now? Or wait until you are in a marriage with a man who is nothing like the man you hoped for? Be aware of the warning signs. If you are suddenly too busy to think through things, if you are avoiding the mirror or any in-depth look at your heart, stop now. Take a deep breath. And think about this relationship. You may even discover that the worries you were avoiding are worries that can be worked through. Wouldn't that be a good thing? Just remember that they may *not* be workable. And it would be better to know now! So I encourage you, if you are noticing a trend toward blind love, take a step back and think. The relationship, and the state of your heart, will be all the better for it.

Half-truths to accountability partners. Do you find yourself telling only a portion of the truth to those who ask you the hard questions? Maybe he has told you something that sent a red flag skyrocketing, but then you kept that information to yourself. *Well,* you may think to yourself, *I know the context in which it was said . . . and he didn't really mean it.* Or perhaps there's a troubling habit that you've noticed. But you don't mention it to anyone else for fear that they will tell you to get out of the relationship.

I noticed this several years ago when a handsome man began to pursue me. There were things that he shared about his past that made me uncomfortable, and I found myself hesitating to share that information with my friends and family. I justified my withholding with different excuses. But if I had been honest with myself, I would have seen immediately that the very fact that I was scared to share the information was a huge red flag. We have to remember that the people who love us want what is best for us. They are a valuable set of eyes to keep us grounded when we are tempted to blind ourselves. We desperately need them to tell us when we are lying to ourselves.

The truth is that whatever we may be ignoring could be the very thing that will cause us tremendous pain later on. There is no momentary pleasure worth the long-term heartache. So, where are you? Are you being honest with the people who care about you? If you're not, why not?

Hiding from God. Melissa didn't really notice how her quiet times were slipping away. Well, she noticed, but she didn't acknowledge it. Whenever the thought swept through her mind, she would pacify herself with the reasoning that it was just temporary. After all, she was staying up later, hanging out on the phone with her new beau, and just didn't have the gumption to wake up at her typical early hour. She knew she would get back into her routine again as soon as life settled down a little bit.

But later on, when Melissa looked back on her justifications, she discovered an uncomfortable truth. The reason that she didn't spend time with God was because she was scared of what He might whisper to her heart. It was the first time in a long time that she had experienced romance in her life, and she didn't want God to say no. She simply wanted to savor and enjoy the experience for the time being. Later on, if He told her no, she would walk away. *But just for a little while*, she had thought to herself, *I want to experience this without reservation.*

The truth: If Melissa was afraid to spend that time with God, then the Holy Spirit was already working in her heart. He was already telling her that the relationship wasn't right. The lie that Melissa believed was that God was withholding something good from her. She forgot that He is out for her best, that He loves her deeply and passionately, and that if He said no, it would be to protect her. This is a lie that many of us encounter. We come out from the shadow of His wing and proceed in a relationship because we long to know love. We may *say* that God is kind and loving, but we are *living* that He is stingy and angry.

Remember that God is the author of all good things, the giver of all good gifts. If He is encouraging us out of a relationship, it is out of His love for us and His desire to protect us from brokenness. What a good and gracious Father we have! He is not withholding pleasure; He is protecting us. If you are finding yourself hiding from God, please draw near. Share with Him your every thought and longing and let Him minister His truth and love to you.

Take Time Away

One of the ways we can be blinded in relationship is if we proceed quickly and intensely. If there is no time apart, beyond work and outside commitments, it's very hard to think rationally. The only thing we tend to think about in that scenario is the time we've just spent with him and the time that's coming up. There is no freedom and objectivity to evaluate the relationship. I would strongly encourage you to take some time away from your relationship on a regular basis. Schedule a date with yourself; take a personal retreat. Even if the relationship is everything you could have hoped for, this time away will give you the perspective that you need.

In addition to gaining perspective, some time away will help you maintain your own identity. What I so often see in my girlfriends and in myself is the tendency to lose our identity in the man we are falling in love with. Suddenly, the things that were once important to us take on a secondary role in our lives. You will respect yourself, and your boyfriend (if he is healthy) will respect you as well, if you remain committed to maintaining your own identity through time away from the relationship.

Know Your Weaknesses

Be aware of the warning signs in yourself that let you know a relationship is unhealthy or becoming so. Often, when we encounter stressful situations, or fall into things that are inappropriate, there are other signs we can take notice of. Perhaps we're falling into old addictions, hiding in areas where we've hid before. Maybe you are withdrawing from friends and family or you notice an irritability that is outside of your character.

There could be any number of things. Try to discern why your weaknesses are surfacing. It could be that the relationship is healthy and that is a scary thing for you. Perhaps you're being vulnerable for the first time in a long time and it's bringing up some of your old hiding places. If that is the case, your response to the relationship will be to remain connected and work hard at hiding in the hand of your heavenly Father as opposed to old habits.

So, you may wonder, *how do I know which it is? Am I hiding because it's good or hiding because it's a bad situation?* Which brings me to my final suggestion:

Pray!

God knows you better than you know yourself. He remembers things that you have long forgotten. He understands your motives, your weaknesses, your fears, your strengths. He is out for your best. Pray. Ask Him for wisdom and discernment. Ask Him for courage where you have once been afraid and for sight where you have once been blind. He is a faithful God who hears our cries. Rather than separating from Him as you begin to experience an earthly set of arms, draw ever closer to the heart that beats for you. He will tell you! He will tell you through His Holy Spirit, through His holy Word, through the nudging in your heart and mind. He will tell you through close Christian friends and family. He will tell you through books and sermons. He does not hide Himself from those who seek Him earnestly. In fact, He promises that if you seek Him, He will be found by you.

Don't leave Him out of the loop in your relationship. Go to Him with everything and let Him teach you how to see the truth. If you doubt this, write down His promises. Find the Scriptures that meet your doubt, that banish your concerns, and memorize them. And please don't forget God is the creator of the marriage relationship. He enjoys blessing His children with good relationships that illustrate His love in dynamic ways. He longs for you to be healthy so that you can experience the best in relationships. If He is saying no, there is a reason. And that reason is for your best. If He is saying yes, it's because as the Author of romance, He desires to bless you with a good gift. But you cannot know whether your relationship is a gift or a hindrance unless you take the time to come to Him in prayer.

When It's Wrong

If God has been whispering to your heart, if friends have been waving the red flags high, if you know somewhere inside that the relationship is not right, you may still remain in the relationship. Why? I believe there are some common lies that we cling to when a relationship has gone sour. Cycle through these typical rationales and see if any of them sound familiar:

"It will get better . . ." If you are at the front end of a relationship and it's not good now, chances are it won't get much better. If there are major differences in belief, in philosophy of life, in personality, if there are things that really irritate you, those things will only grow in significance. I can remember a friend saying to me, "Elsa, if that's upsetting you now, when the music is playing and the romance is sweet, it will only upset you further when the relationship deepens to the discussion of toothpaste-squeezing and the positioning of toilet paper rolls."

Obviously, no human being is perfect. We all have our quirks and irritating habits. What you have to decide is if that particular habit is one you can live with if it gets worse. That's what you have to assume, that the things that irritate you will become glaring and the things that enchant you will diminish in their prevalence. I don't mean to sound pessimistic, but it's really the truth. Intimate relationships bring out the best and the worst in us.

Looking at your partner, are you willing to go the distance with him? I would encourage you to look at it this way. If the thing that is making you uncomfortable is a character issue, be very, very careful. If he lies, cheats, steals, leans toward unfaithfulness, these things will destroy a relationship. If he happens to chew his fingernails or isn't as neat as you would like, those are things that can be worked through. But don't assume any of these issues will get better. They may, but they may not. Decide if you can deal with those things now.

"It's better than nothing . . ." For many women, it is the fear of being alone that has kept them in horrible relationships. A dear friend of mine was terrified that she would never know love if she got out of her current relationship. Not that she knew love in the relationship she was in, but at least he was there. And that was better than being alone. The fear of being alone has robbed so many women of the potential for good relationships. If this is you, if you are staying in this relationship because it is better than being alone, please reconsider. Start building connections and friendships outside of your dating relationship. Get involved in a small group, seek counseling, do whatever it takes to change this particular mindset. Being in a poor relationship can rob you of so much! God has so much more for you—lean into Him, ask Him to help you break free. He will hear your cry!

"I'll do it after . . ." "After that wedding we're supposed to go to . . ." "After his mother gets better . . ." "After he finds that job . . ." "After I get on my feet . . ." The relationship lingers and lingers and lingers as we put off its demise until the next event has passed. After Christmas. After the New Year. After Spring Break. Suddenly, you look back to discover that you've lost two or three years of your life to a relationship that is all wrong. Now. Now is the time to end it.

There is never an ideal moment to do the hard thing. It will never be easier or more convenient than it is right now. And remember, the longer you are in a relationship that is broken, the longer it will take to heal as you grieve the loss. Today, not tomorrow. If you know that it isn't right, take the steps now. It will save you pain, save him pain, save you precious time, and it is simply the honorable thing to do! If you are in a relationship that you know isn't right, it dishonors you, your date, and God.

Think how good it will feel to make the right choice, even if it is the harder one. And don't do it alone. Gather friends around you and ask them to pray for the strength that you will need. Make sure you plan some things with them as well for after the break-up. Lean on others and allow them to be there for you. You *can* do this.

"But he loves me . . ." I imagine there are books and books devoted to understanding this line of thinking. Here's my take on it from some of my own experiences. In some of my old relationships, I felt an odd obligation to return the love of someone who cared for me. It was almost as though I loved him simply because he loved me, not because of who he was as a man. It was certainly a sign of my own lack of value. In my mind, I returned his love because he was kind enough to love me. So I owed him something. All of me. Maybe you've experienced this. If so, I want to share with you a truth that I have learned: You don't owe him for loving you. You are not so hard to love that, if he does, you must pay him back with your undying devotion.

You are a handcrafted, beautifully designed treasure in the eyes of your God. If you are suffering from this particular perspective, I have an assignment for you. Seek out your identity in Christ. And do that with people you trust. If you're anything like me, the feeling is deeply ingrained. It's not something that will change overnight because you decide it should. It requires some work.

For me, it took counseling, friends to consistently remind me of His heart, and reading good books that taught me how to replace the lies with God's truth. Oh, but it can be done, and the work is worth it! There is no desperation when you understand how valuable you are to God. There is no sense of obligation when you are resting in the identity He grants you. With that identity comes a freedom to love because of who your beau is, not for how his love defines you.

How to Say It

I could simply direct you to my past and say, "Don't do it that way!" This has not been my strongest suit. I've let someone go only to call them the next week. I've stumbled over my words, I've waited far too long, I've done it all possible ways except the right way. Yet I've learned. And perhaps it took learning all the wrong ways to begin to understand the honorable way to walk away. Here are a few ideas that I've gleaned from wiser women than I and truths I have learned through my own mistakes:

Say it straight . . . Beating around the bush in a thousand different ways does absolutely nothing but confuse the relationship. "I think I might be scared . . . possibly . . . and I might be backing away . . . but it's not your fault or anything. By the way, are you doing anything tomorrow night?" It's very hard to pacify a hurt while inflicting it. We can certainly qualify our statements by saying things like, "I don't want to hurt you, but this relationship isn't working." Or, "I think you are a good man, but I know my weaknesses, and this relationship isn't bringing out the best in either one of us. We need to end it." You can encase it in kind truth, but to say everything except that you need to end the relationship will hurt you both.

Say it. Be straight. The amazing thing is you will find a delight in your inner strength. It will be difficult to be completely honest, but it will strengthen both of you if you are able to do it. Also, if you can, give a reason that will be helpful to the person receiving it. "I need to break things off because you have been dishonest with me several times. I need to know that I can trust you, and right now I can't." Stating the reason for the break-up can be a growing experience for the both of you.

If he does lie, it would be good for him to know that there are relational consequences to that kind of behavior. Or it may be something in you: "I notice that I get extremely jealous and I know that doesn't honor God or you. I need to take a break from this relationship so that I can figure out where that fear comes from." Whatever the scenario might be, tell it to him straight. He may get angry in the moment, but ultimately, if he is reasonably healthy, he will appreciate your honesty.

Say it in a safe place. I would have the conversation in a public place. Meet him somewhere for dinner, talk over lunch, but stay away from intimate environments. It would be difficult to end the relationship when you are cuddling on the couch.

Respect. Maybe in order to end the relationship, you feel like you need to dig into every past painful experience. It might even be tempting to bring up all that he has ever done, to end the relationship on angry terms in order to avoid the pain. Don't do it. As much as it is up to you, treat him with respect. Tell him the truth and tell it to him graciously.

Give the relationship space. "But I would like to stay friends." We've all heard the line and probably said it several times ourselves. It could happen. A good friendship could come from a dating relationship, but not right away. Give both of you the appropriate time to grieve and readjust to the new status of your relationship. Expecting an immediate friendship will lead to one of two things. Either you'll end up back in the dating relationship, or you'll continue to open a wound that needs time to scab over and heal. Give it time.

Bottom Line

In each of the other chapters, we have closed out the chapter with questions. We won't do that for this or the next chapter. You know, in your heart, if this is something you need to address in your relationship. And if any of these points have resonated for you, I pray that you will take the necessary steps to walk away from your beau. Remember that there is no easy way to end a dating relationship. Yet there are ways to make the process easier. Lean on your heavenly Father, ask friends for prayer and encouragement, be straight with your dating partner, treat him with respect, and give each other space.

Chapter Ten

How to Stay When It's Right

Sarah thought that John might be a man she could marry. He was so much of what she longed for, and their relationship was sweet and fulfilling. She was scared, though. She'd been through some tough relationships in the past, and she wanted to make sure that she handled this one well, honoring both God and John. They'd been dating for three months and she wasn't sure what their next step would be. She tried not to think about it too much and instead did her best to rest in her Lord's care. Yet she couldn't help wondering, were they going to make it? Were his feelings growing as well? Should she show more interest or let John dictate the course of their relationship? What did he expect? What did she expect?

There were so many questions that chased each other through her mind. She wished she didn't worry so much and that she had a blueprint on how to handle her concerns. This was one relationship she didn't want to damage by her relational immaturity. "Oh Lord," she prayed, "help me to please You in this relationship. Teach me how to move forward in a way that blesses You . . . how I long for that!"

What Now?

Perhaps you've felt some of the same fears and concerns that Sarah experienced. I know that I have. There are times I've driven myself crazy with a frenzy of questions that aren't easily answered. How can we best set ourselves up for success? What steps can we take that will honor our God and our beau? This chapter is dedicated to sharing tools that will help you in this process. I'm making one large assumption, though. I'm assuming that you are dating a godly man, that you are comfortable with his character, and that the relationship has the real potential for success. If this describes you, or where you hope to be in a dating relationship, then read on . . .

Define Expectations

My friend Denise sat me down. "Okay, you're dating. What does that mean to you?" I looked at her, thought for a moment, shrugged my shoulders and finally spoke. "I think it means that we're getting to know each other, becoming friends, spending time together." "How much time?" she asked me. I shrugged again. "I mean," she paused, "are you going to get together once a week? Twice a week? Are you going to talk every day? What does dating mean to you?"

I was stuck. I had never really defined the dating process in my mind. What did it look like? And what if my perception of dating was completely different from that of the man I was seeing? They were good questions and were extremely helpful as I looked at my relationship. I began to see that dating in my mind might be completely different than dating in his mind.

What is your expectation of a dating relationship? What is his? Are you exclusive? (Something I highly recommend.) Will you see each other once every couple of weeks? Once a week? If your expectation is completely different from his, you may be in store for some disappointment. I think it would be helpful to define this early on in the relationship. Now obviously, you are not going to lay it all out there on the first date. But if the relationship is progressing, it is important to understand each other's internal expectations. One word of caution, though: When you share your expectations and ask about his, make it clear that you simply desire to avoid disappointment on both ends. If you lay your expectation out there and then demand that it be met, that will hinder the relationship. Be open and willing to experience dating in new ways.

Engaging in Relationship

What does it look like to truly commit to and grow in a relationship? How do we take responsible risks and move forward in a godly manner? I want to take you directly to God's Word to answer these questions. 1 Corinthians 13 is a familiar passage to most of us—it's the "love" chapter. We are going to take a closer look at Paul's definition of real love, applying God's truth to our dating relationships.

Love is patient, love is kind. It does not envy, it does not boast, it is not proud. It is not rude, it is not self-seeking, it is not easily angered, it keeps no record of wrongs. Love does not delight in evil but rejoices with the truth. It always protects, always trusts, always hopes, always perseveres.
—1 Corinthians 13:4–7

Perhaps the word *love* scares you a little bit. Maybe you're thinking, *Wait a minute, I'm just dating this man. I'm not sure if I love him yet!* That's okay. You don't have to know for certain that you love him, but remember I'm making the assumption that you are in a growing relationship with a godly man. Or that at some point you long to be in that kind of relationship. These principles apply across the board because they are the rules of intimacy. And dating, by nature, is intimate.

Be patient. We're women of the new millennium. We're aggressive and confident. We know what we want and we know how to get it. These are the themes of our culture, the definition of *woman*. What does that mean for our relationships? Confusion. There is part of us that longs to be swept off of our feet, romanced by the perfect gentleman, protected, and cherished. There is another part of us that has been trained to resist such behavior. I can open my own door! I can call him! If I want to ask a man out, I will! I am woman!

I'm as independent as any woman is. I support and provide for my family, mow the lawn, change the oil in my car (well okay, I drive it to the nearest place that can), and lead various ministry groups. But when it comes to relationship, I believe that God set it up for the man to take the lead. As self-sufficient and independent as I am, I am still very willing to allow the man to define the relationship and move it forward.

Think of the ways that God has pursued the church, giving His life up for her. He defines the marriage relationship in the same terms (Eph. 5:25–32). It's okay to be pursued; it's good to be pursued. If you are longing for a man who has the ability and the strength to be a spiritual leader after marriage, someone who will protect and cover his family with honor, then he has to have the freedom to pursue you in the dating relationship. And this is where patience comes in.

Janet was excited when she met Dan. He was handsome and godly, a true gentleman. They began dating and she felt good about her level-headedness. Yet several months into the relationship, Dan slowed his pursuit. As it turned out, his work had taken on a new level of intensity and he'd also been increasing his prayer time in regard to the relationship. Janet wondered about the smaller number of calls, immediately assuming it was something she had done. Inwardly, she started to panic and began calling him instead. *He's probably waiting on my call*, she thought to herself.

Slowly, the relationship turned a corner. Janet was the pursuer and Dan the pursued. Rather than rest in the hand of her God, who always had her best in mind, instead of resting in the trust that had already been established in their dating relationship, Janet took matters into her own hands. Her insecurity made Dan uncomfortable and in time, with regret, he made the decision to end the relationship.

My encouragement to you, my dear friend, is to trust that you are worthy of pursuit. Trust that God has things in control and rest in His hand. Be patient in the dating process. If God has ordained that the two of you are meant to be a team, He will lay that on your partner's heart as well. Rest. Wait. Be patient. And enjoy the sweet pleasure of being pursued.

Be kind. This one is almost a no-brainer. And most women don't have a lot of trouble with this. We have been raised to nurture, to give of ourselves, to be kind. What does kindness look like in a relationship? Perhaps it's listening, writing a note of encouragement, being supportive. It might look like friendship. How do we treat our best girlfriends? What kindness do we offer them? Are we as kind to the man we are dating?

Do a motives check. Are you being kind because you care for him? Because he is a good man and you desire to bring a smile to his face? Or are you being kind because it makes you look like a wonderful human being (i.e. potential wife?). I ask that with tongue in cheek because so often in my past, that was exactly my motive! I was kind to make me look good, to make him long for me.

Obviously, we all have a mixed bag of motives. There may be a little of both of those motives in your acts of kindness. Just be self-aware. And if you find yourself going out of your way simply to make him swoon, dig around inside to discover why. You may be depending on him to define your value, or you may not believe that you are deserving of love without earning it first. Be kind because it's the right thing to do and he deserves it.

If your motives are questionable, you have an opportunity to acknowledge it, address it, and grow through to the other side. And that's a good thing!

Love doesn't envy. What does envy look like in a dating relationship? I think of outside relationships. Both you and your dating partner need to encourage each other in your outside relationships. Give each other the freedom to spend time with friends, family, and accountability partners.

Most often, envy plays out in a relationship in the form of time. We long for more time with the one we are dating and we envy the time he spends doing other things. Think of it this way. You can't fulfill every need that your boyfriend has. He needs his male friends, his leisure pursuits, and his own growth environments. When he is freed up to enjoy those, he can engage in relationship with you. He'll have more to give and he'll be happier giving it because he has enjoyed refreshment in other areas. It is good to support and encourage outside relationships and interests.

Love doesn't boast. When I think of this one, it makes me laugh. I can remember, as a teenager, boasting beyond measure to potential loves. I would share things that made me look like Wonder Woman, Betty Crocker, and Joan of Arc all rolled into one. I could cook, clean, organize, bungee-jump, motorcycle race . . . whatever. The truth is, I'm an okay cook. I'm not so good on the organization front, either. I actually do like to bungee-jump and ride motorcycles, but I don't race them. Sometimes in our effort to put our best foot forward, we exaggerate our strengths and downplay our weaknesses. Some of that is natural; we want to expose only our best side. Just be careful. Don't make yourself out to be Outdoor Woman Extraordinaire when you hate the very thought of sleeping under the stars with creepy bugs and critters. Don't say you've been on every roller coaster ever made when you turned green on the ferris wheel just last summer. And if you can't cook, don't order in fancy stuff and say that you made it from scratch. Be honest about your likes and dislikes, talents and gifts. Boasting in regard to things that you truly can't do will lead only to disappointment.

Love is not rude. I've seen people settle into a relationship and suddenly lose all sense of courtesy. They don't say please, they show up late, they give each other glaring looks. Rudeness is unacceptable no matter what relationship you're in. Always treat your date with respect. Be gracious.

Love is not proud. No one likes to be wrong. Here's the catch: We're all wrong sometimes. As a broken people living in a fallen world, we are going to make mistakes. Knowing that is half the battle. When you make a blunder in your relationship—maybe lying about being Outdoor Woman Extraordinaire, or inadvertently dropping his antique vase that's been around for a thousand generations, or even snapping rudely when you meant to ask kindly—'fess up. Don't give excuses, rationales (i.e. the old PMS backup excuse). Simply apologize; acknowledge that you made a mistake and move on. In scenarios like these, it's best to remember how you like to be treated. If he makes a mistake, wouldn't you rather have an apology than an excuse or a nine-point line of defense? It's okay. Whether we believe it or not, it's true. Nobody is perfect.

Not self-seeking. What does it look like to be self-seeking in a relationship? I think we seek ourselves when we avoid depth in our relationships. If you are entering into this dating relationship fully protected and unwilling to be vulnerable, you are protecting yourself above all else. You are self-seeking. Pieter VanWaarde, my brother and a pastor in my town, recently did a series on building relationships. He spoke on the importance of relational risk, and I want to share some of his thoughts here:

When it comes to relating to other people, there can be a dualism inside that paralyzes us. On one side, we are convinced that this [relationship] is probably not going to go well, so why even try—the fear of what has been. Then, on the other side, we long for a measure of intimacy, for without it we feel empty and unfulfilled—the fear of what might be.

So what do we do?

I would suggest that many people do nothing. They get stuck right there in the middle. They live out their lives, making excuses for why their relationships will never work. They allow the pains of their own pasts and the ample evidence of relational breakdowns (which are all around them) to keep them from moving beyond the walls they have built up around themselves. They continue to stuff down the desire for intimacy. In the process, they decide to live life without ever really experiencing what God designed us for—meaningful, life-giving relationships on multiple levels. In addition, they pay another price for doing nothing. That price is paid on two levels:

One: We miss out on the good God designed for us in relationship. Around the church, we typically emphasize being rightly related to God, which is essential. But there is another part to God's plan, which has to do with how we relate to one another. Jesus, when He was asked about the most important commandment, responded by saying,

"The most important one," answered Jesus, "is this: 'Hear, O Israel, the Lord our God, the Lord is one. Love the Lord your God with all your heart and with all your soul and with all your mind and with all your strength.' The second is this: 'Love your neighbor as yourself.' There is no commandment greater than these." —Mark 12:29–31

Now, why is it important to God that we love each other? Why would that be a command? I think first of all that God knew how hard it would be to do it. And unless He commanded it, we probably wouldn't go there. Yet, perhaps there is another reason that Jesus said it so strongly: He knew how good it is when people really take the time and energy to love each other!

Think of the times in your life when you have really connected to another human being. Whether it was a friend, a parent, a sibling, or a boyfriend. Wasn't there a joy to that kind of intimacy that was irreplaceable? How good would it feel to know that kind of joy in your current relationship? Yes, there will be bumps along the way, times of awkwardness, and even some rejection. But you can't let fear keep you from investigating how good it is to taste the goodness that the Lord has for you in deeper and more satisfying relationships.

Two: We become susceptible to significant dysfunction. For some, the prospect of deep personal relationships isn't all that attractive. So the potential loss of relationship doesn't seem like a big issue. The assumption is that missing the potential good side is all that's at stake. Yet that is not the case. The price of not engaging is not just that we miss out on something good. We also open ourselves up to something bad.

When we choose to reject the pursuit of meaningful relationships, it leaves a hole in our soul. We may not admit that it is there. We may not even be able to identify it—we just know something is not exactly right on the inside. And make no mistake about it; this hole intends to be filled with something. It's this hole that prompts addictions to pornography, sexual dysfunction, and compulsive behaviors. We long to be filled, and if we are not being filled first by our God and then by relationship, we will find something else to pour into our souls.

Remember when we are self-seeking, when we are doing our very best to preserve our hearts from damage, we are missing out on God's relational blessings and opening ourselves up to dysfunction. Be willing to risk.

Let me share one more thought on that, something that has helped me tremendously in opening my own heart to risk: Be settled in your first love. If God is your first love, no break-up can destroy your heart. If He is your everything, you will be free to love others without the risk of losing it all. Remember that there is security in His hand.

Not easily angered. Don't allow yourself to be easily irritated. Remember that you are entering into a relationship with someone who has lived a long time without you. They are going to have habits and mannerisms that are their own. They will have a way of doing things that might not look anything like the way you do things. Keep that in mind and reserve your anger for the things that matter.

Keeps no record of wrongs. Remember our discussion on being proud? How important it is to 'fess up and admit when we are wrong? It's just as important to let things go when we have forgiven our beau. Keeping a long list of past transgressions and then listing them off with each new transgression is bound to damage any relationship. Let the past remain in the past and deal with the current issue.

Does not delight in evil. Let's just say that you have a bad habit or two. You're trying to break their hold on your life, but it's been a rough road. Now imagine that you discover that your beau has similar bad habits. Does that bring a smile to your face? Obviously we all have our struggles, but don't ever delight in the struggles of your man, even if it makes facing your own struggles easier.

And just a thought on this: if he is struggling with the exact same issues as you are—for example, you both battle compulsive overeating—you might be in for a hard journey. It may be easy for both of you to slip into that pattern of behavior because you may be tempted to justify it to one another. Another area where you may delight in evil is in the physical realm. If you are hoping to tempt him, to push the limits, and then if you feel victorious when you get to that point, that would fall into this category. Encourage your beau towards godliness as you pursue the same.

Rejoices with the truth. Celebrate each other's successes, even if it means that the relationship may experience some hardship. I think again of the physical boundaries. There may be some mixed emotions that come when your boyfriend leaves you standing at the door without so much as a kiss. Rejoice in his values; celebrate the fact that you are dating a godly man! Or perhaps he is tithing ten percent and doesn't have the money for extravagant dates; that's something we should look at with God's heart. Or maybe it's something that has nothing to do with your relationship. Maybe he's simply made a good choice or followed God's will in some area of his life. Enjoy that in him, celebrate it!

Always protects. I think of this principle as protecting each other's reputation. My friend Denise tells of the time when her boyfriend Ken was leaving town to attend a high school reunion. They'd been dating for some time and Denise wanted to go with him. Even though she planned on getting a separate hotel room, Ken declined. He didn't want anyone within their circle of friends to think they had crossed physical boundaries. He was very protective of her reputation and went to great lengths to protect it. This plays out in other areas as well. It's how you speak of him when not in his presence. It's defending him if the need arises or honoring his heart by the way we treat him. Hopefully, he is doing the same for you. What an incredible thing—to protect and be protected!

Always trusts. Janie didn't believe him. Her boyfriend Alan told her that he needed some time away to figure out the future of his career. She thought it was something else. She believed he was just making an excuse to get out of the relationship. She spent the next few weeks angry and sullen over his withdrawal. And when he came back, with a smile on his face and open arms, she felt embarrassed. She'd spent all that time arguing with him in her mind, deciding that maybe she didn't like him after all, only to discover that he had been telling her the truth.

It's important that we trust our boyfriends. Of course, most of us have been through experiences where our trust has been betrayed. Yet just like we discussed in the section on self-seeking, at some point we have to choose to

---

believe. Yes, he might not be telling the truth, and we may be hurt. But on the other hand, he might be honest and honorable and a genuinely trustworthy man. Committing to a relationship means committing to the person and trusting that he will be honest with us.

Always hopes. I believe that hoping in a relationship is about believing the best about the relationship and about the man. When we've been hurt in the past, we tend to jump to negative conclusions based on little evidence. Believe the best!

Always perseveres. Does the first sign of conflict send you running for the hills? Relationships are hard! There are so many adjustments to be made, so much understanding to give and receive, so much effort! Sometimes we may wonder if it's even worth it. But if you are in a solid relationship with a godly man, it's worth fighting for. Stick through the tough moments, especially after the early "life is amazing, my guy is amazing, everything is amazing" feeling that we experience in the first months. With time comes the exposure of weaknesses, disagreements, and even disillusionment. This is the time, if your man is one of character and integrity, when you should fight through to the other side. Persevere. Don't give up.

My friend, I'm not naïve enough to think that you were able to absorb each and every one of these points and will now be able to incorporate each of them into your relationship. In fact, I imagine that most of them resonated with what you already knew. What I do hope for is that there was one or two that especially applied to your particular relationship. Perhaps you struggle with trusting your boyfriend, or maybe you have a problem risking the deeper parts of yourself. If you experienced any triggers as you read through the above list, I pray that you will pursue it. Find out how you can improve in that area and allow God to use this little nudge as a launching pad for growth.

The stronger you are in a dating relationship, the stronger your marriage will be. There are so many good books available in each of the areas I've mentioned. Find them, read them, grow. It will bless God, bless you, and bless your relationship.

When Children Are Involved

I am a single parent; many of you may be as well. When there are children involved, how do we protect their hearts? I want to make a suggestion. Don't introduce your child to your dating partner until the relationship is serious. At that point, introduce them in a safe environment. Do things with several other people so that your child is comfortable. Allow them to get to know your boyfriend without pressure.

When you're with that group, make sure you refrain from physical contact. That kind of contact can feel threatening to a child. There's no need to hold hands or clutch each other around the waist. Imagine how that feels to the child! Suddenly there is someone else with you, and the child may feel like she is on the outside. For that reason, keep the physical contact to a minimum. Finally, give your child time to adjust to this new development. They haven't had to share you and the prospect probably isn't that pleasing now. Be sensitive to that and be willing to give them time.

My Prayer for You

When I started writing this book, I prayed that it would be a valuable tool in the hands of the women who read it. I wanted, more than anything, to resist fluffy concepts. My intent has been to give practical advice to those in dating relationships, who are preparing for marriage as God intends. For that reason, I want to finish the book with a prayer, asking God for exactly that.

Sweet Heavenly Father,

I am so grateful that You are the Author of love and the Creator of relationship. What rich blessings they have the potential to be! I pray, Lord, that every woman who reads this book would discover biblical truth that they can apply to their relationships. On the flip side, I ask that anything that is not of You would float away like chaff. Bless their relationships, Father; protect their hearts while encouraging them to risk. Bring them joy and confidence in their relationship with You so that they can freely love another. Grant them wisdom and discernment so that they might know when to stay and when to go. And Lord, if the relationship isn't right, give them the courage to walk away. You are the Giver of all good gifts; may these women experience Your generosity in their romantic relationships. And may they know deep intimacy, joyful connection, and true companionship with a godly man.

In Jesus' name, Amen!

Also by Elsa Kok

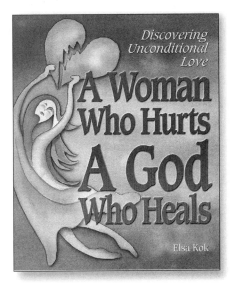

1-56309-708-7

If you're one of the thousands of women who struggle with feelings of shame or exclusion because of your past and hurtful romantic relationships, this book is for you. It will meet you right where you are, and you don't need any Bible knowledge to begin.

This study is excellent in helping us move beyond the pain of our past and into healing and wholeness.
—NANCY ALCORN, FOUNDER,
MERCY MINISTRIES OF AMERICA

AVAILABLE IN BOOKSTORES EVERYWHERE.

New Hope Publishers

Equipping You to Share the Hope of Christ